Inside Publishing

The Bobbs-Merrill Company, Inc.
Indianapolis/New York

Published by The Bobbs-Merrill Company, Inc.
Indianapolis/New York

Library of Congress Cataloging in Publication Data

Adler, Bill.
Inside publishing.

1. Publishers and publishing. 2. Book industries and
trade. I. Title.

Z278.A3 070.5 81-17978
ISBN 0-672-52680-8 AACR2

Designed by MARY A. BROWN
Manufactured in the United States of America

First Printing

*I am most grateful to Julie Rosner
and Betty Alexander whose
assistance and judgment helped
make this book possible.*

To *Gloria*
My partner in life and in business

CONTENTS

Foreword

I have put it all down as I see it and as I know it. This is a subjective book but it is also the result of more than twenty years in book publishing as a writer, editor, book packager and agent.

Above all, I have tried to be honest with myself and I hope I have not stepped on too many toes.

To quote my good friend and client, Howard Cosell, I have tried to tell it "like it is"—I have not held back nor have I concerned myself with the fact that some people may be upset by this book and others may not be too thrilled.

This is not a book about publishing alone but a book about the people in publishing for, in actuality, publishing is a people business. It is filled with fascinating characters, brilliant entrepreneurs and more than one person who is a little off the wall. That's what makes it so exciting.

This was my best shot about the business and I hope, if nothing else, that the people who write, make and publish books come alive in these pages.

BILL ADLER
New York City

1

So You Want to Be an Author

IN order to be a successful engineer, you have to have the proper educational background. If you want to become a lawyer, a degree from a law school is a prerequisite. Success in the corporate business world demands knowledge of the industry in which you are working plus experience and background.

There is one endeavor, however, that is open to everyone and the only prerequisite is that you be able to write (and you don't even have to write that well).

Every year more than 30,000 hardcover books are published in the United States making many men and women wealthy overnight.

The publishing industry is filled with stories of men and women who have written everything from cookbooks to books on how to cure backaches to racy first novels that have become overnight sensations and have earned hundreds of thousands of dollars for their authors.

Before I tell you how practically anyone can get published if he has the strong desire and determination, I would like to present one case history that perhaps best dramatizes the golden opportunities available in book publishing.

Francine Prince is a Manhattan housewife and mother who has a passion for cooking. In 1974 her husband, Harold, suffered a severe heart attack and Francine decided that the best thing to do toward rehabilitating Harold's health was to change his diet.

And she did exactly that. She began cooking for her husband and herself without salt or sugar, and yet she was determined that the food she served would still be as tasty as it had been prior to Harold's heart attack.

When Francine began serving her newly developed recipes to friends the comments were always the same:

"It's delicious."

"It's so tasty."

"Where did you get the recipe?"

One day, Francine and Harold Prince decided that perhaps they could publish their new recipes in a book titled *The Dieter's Gourmet Cookbook.* They didn't have an agent (although subsequently my company represented them) so they began knocking on the doors of book publishers. They received many rejections and encountered much lack of interest from many of the publishers they approached.

One of the first rules for succeeding in book publishing is determination. If you believe in your own project or manuscript, you should not permit others to talk you out of it with their negative reaction.

Finally, after months of frustrating rejections, Francine Prince found a publisher—Norman Monath, president of Cornerstone Library, who was interested in publishing *The Dieter's Gourmet Cookbook.* He offered them a small advance of $3,000 and an average royalty of 7½% on every copy sold (a standard royalty for a trade paperback).

The Dieter's Gourmet Cookbook has been an enormous success. It has sold over 100,000 copies, first at $4.95 and later at $6.95, and has earned to date royalties in excess of $50,000 for Francine Prince.

The success of *The Dieter's Gourmet Cookbook* has led to additional successful books by Francine Prince. Her second book, published by Cornerstone Library and represented by my agency, was titled *Diet for Life* and has sold more than 50,000 copies, earning about $50,000 for its author.

Francine Prince has become what is known in the book trade as a "property," which means that her name has commercial value in bookstores and with the public. As a result she now has contracts for four additional books for which the total advance payments will be close to $100,000.

You can therefore readily see that from a small advance of $3,000 originally paid by Cornerstone Library for Francine Prince's first book, she has now earned in excess of $200,000. Not bad for a woman who had never been published before and who developed her expertise in the kitchen into a profitable enterprise for herself and her family.

There are many stories like Francine Prince's—stories of men and women who have had no professional experience as writers but have relied on their knowledge in a particular field to write books which make considerable amounts of money.

If you want to get published, either because you have an idea or a manuscript or an outline for a book, how do you go about it?

The most important thing to understand about book publishing is that it is a printed medium.

When people call me at my office to say that they would like "to tell me about their book," I always reply in the same manner: "Don't *tell* me about your book. Book publishing is a printed medium. Let me *see* something on paper." If you want to get published, you must have something written first—either a substantial outline or the completed manuscript.

If you are going to submit an outline to a publisher or agent (we'll discuss later how to get a publisher or agent), then the outline should accomplish two things.

It should clearly describe the idea for the book you have in mind.

It should present a good example of how the book will be written.

It is a golden rule in book publishing that no idea will make it unless it is executed properly or written well.

If Francine Prince had not prepared her manuscript for *The Dieter's Gourmet Cookbook* well, I would not now be writing about her success. Or, if Mary Ellen Pinkham had not prepared a good manuscript for her bestseller, *Mary Ellen's Best of Helpful Hints,* the book probably would never have been published; and if it had been published it would have undoubtedly failed. But like Francine Prince, Mary Ellen executed her manuscript well, and that made the difference.

There are many publishers who will not buy first books by an unknown author unless they have a completed manuscript (this is especially true in fiction). Each publisher and each editor has different requirements but as a general rule, the more material you can present to a publisher, the better your chances are for getting a contract.

We usually recommend to authors who are writing their first book that they submit an outline and at least a sample chapter. In the case of

Francine Prince's book, she actually submitted the completed manuscript to the publisher.

There are many kinds of book proposals, and they differ in length and approach depending upon the writer and the subject of the book. If the author has a track record then the proposal can be simple and more to the point, but if the author is more of an unknown quantity then his or her proposal or outline will have to be more extensive.

The important thing for a writer to remember about a book proposal is that it is essentially a selling tool. It is what determines if the publisher will buy the book and for what price. It is also important to understand that in most situations the book proposal or outline will have to be read by more than one person. Unless you are dealing with the president of the publishing firm or someone else who can make a decision without consulting with anyone, you can safely assume that your proposal will be read by at least two people.

I don't believe outlines should be too wordy or unnecessarily long, but the key to a good outline is the way it describes the book and convinces the editor that this is a book he should publish. The first few sentences of the proposal should quickly and succinctly summarize the thrust or theme of the book.

For instance: "We are proposing a book about the relationship between Abraham Lincoln and General Ulysses S. Grant." Those few words immediately tell the editor what the general theme of the book is all about. The rest of the proposal should describe the book in more detail and in the case of a book about Lincoln and Grant, the author should indicate what research materials he will draw upon to substantiate a book about two major figures from American history.

A nonfiction book proposal should be in three sections:

1. A general description of the book.
2. A detailed breakdown of the proposed chapters for the book (if possible).
3. A description of the author and his qualifications for writing the book.

The outline should not, however, read like a laundry list with one- or two-line descriptions of the book and one-line chapter headings without further amplification. The amplification is necessary so that the publisher can have a sense of the style of the writing that will be in the book.

Included in the Appendix is an outline that worked—an outline that succeeded in getting a contract for the author.

If the writer is represented by an agent, the agent's "sell" letter that accompanies the book proposal is also important. The agent in his letter will usually indicate to the publisher why he believes the book will work and why he thinks the author has the talent to make the book work.

I can't speak for all agents' sell letters since I haven't seen all of them; but I do know that when I was represented by Scott Meredith, I thought his letters were inspired, and I know that within the industry Meredith's sales letters are considered among the best, if not the best.

Some authors make the mistake of thinking that their outline or book proposal should be 90 percent selling copy and 10 percent information about the book. That's a mistake. You don't have to present voluminous statistics and facts on why the book will sell.

"This book on exercise for pregnant women has a big market because there are approximately 3,600,000 pregnant women every year" or "the market for cat books is enormous with more than 23 million registered cat owners in the U.S. (according to the ASPCA)" is sufficient.

If you have never written a book before, an editor may want to see a sample chapter before offering a contract for your nonfiction book. Try to select a chapter that best captures the flavor of the book. Like the outline, the sample chapter should be your best foot forward.

Preparing a book proposal for a novel requires more work, especially if you are a first-time novelist or if your credentials have not yet been firmly established. You may have to write half the novel or, in some cases, the entire novel before being offered a book contract.

The superstars of fiction can, of course, secure a substantial book contract with a brief outline and in some cases with no outline at all.

Unless you are proposing a book that relies heavily on photographs or illustrations, it isn't really necessary to submit the illustrations at the same time that you present the outline or the proposal. Prospective authors are often too concerned initially about the pictures or illustrations that go with a manuscript. I have frequently had authors say to me, "Would you like to see the illustrations for my book now?" and my reply is usually the same, "The manuscript is what most publishers are concerned about first."

Fancy paper or a leather binding for your manuscript or an unusual typeface doesn't help to sell a book proposal, but neatness and legibility do help. If your proposal is too difficult to read because it is filled with typos or has coffee stains all over it—that could affect your sale.

Also, try not to submit a carbon copy of your outline or sample chapters. Carbons are too difficult to read and editors are like the rest of us—if it is too difficult, they would prefer not to make the effort. Instead of submitting a carbon, present the publisher with a clean Xerox copy. If the Xerox is clean and readable, it isn't necessary to submit the original copy. If, however, you insist on presenting the original, make sure you have made a copy for yourself. Most agents will Xerox copies for you (especially the big agents) but they will charge you for the copies.

If you are preparing an outline or proposal for a book that will be stronger with endorsements (medical and self-help books fall into this category), then try to have some of the endorsements when you make the submission. It will help.

If your proposal has been around, make sure that it doesn't look like twenty-five other people have already looked at it. I can recall on more than one occasion when I was the editorial director of the book division of *Playboy* receiving outlines that looked as if they had been typed in 1929. A tattered and shopworn outline is the kiss of death. Every editor likes to think he is looking at a proposal first.

The title for your book—at least the final title—isn't necessary when you submit the proposal because very few books are bought on title alone. You should, of course, title your outline but don't feel that it will necessarily be the final title for your book.

Once you have the idea for your book and once you have written the outline and the sample chapter or even the completed manuscript, what next?

Obviously, you want a publisher. And the question, of course, is how are you going to get one? In my judgment the best way to secure the attention of a publisher for your proposed book is through a literary agent.

Most of the literary agents are in New York and their names, addresses and phone numbers are listed in the yearly publication called the *Literary Market Place* or the *LMP* published by R. R. Bowker Company.

A copy of the *LMP* can be purchased directly from R. R. Bowker (1180 Avenue of the Americas, New York, N.Y. 10036) or you can undoubtedly find a copy at your local library.

Unfortunately there is a "Catch 22" attached to getting a literary agent, and that is that not every literary agent is anxious to take on authors who have not been published before. However, persistence is again the key.

Your first step should be to write literary agents listed in the *LMP*. You certainly could call a literary agent to tell him or her about your project, but as we mentioned earlier an agent is going to want to see the material before making a decision.

Literary agents charge a commission of between 10% and 15% (depending on the agent) and they may want you to sign a contract with them before they agree to represent your book. We strongly suggest that before you sign a contract with any literary agent you have an attorney look over the agreement.

A literary agent's commission is based on the amount of money you earn from the publication of your book. If you make $100,000, a literary agent who charges 10% will make $10,000. The more you make, the more your agent makes.

Up until a few years ago, virtually all literary agents charged a commission of 10%, but recently some of the established agents have been charging 12% or 15%.

If you are fortunate enough to be taken on as a client by a literary agent, then obviously your chances of securing a publisher are greatly enhanced. Most publishers prefer to deal with agents because they feel that the materials submitted to them by agents are likely to be more professional and more publishable than manuscripts that arrive without an agent. In addition, most publishers prefer to negotiate contracts with agents since the agent's expertise makes it easier for the publisher and the author to arrive at a reasonable agreement.

Book publishing is not much different from any other industry—it is not only *what* you know but *who* you know, and literary agents certainly do know editors and publishers and deal with them daily.

In my opinion, the commission charged by literary agents is well worth it, not only because they can more readily obtain a publisher for you but because of their expertise in negotiating a contract on your behalf.

If you are unable to interest a literary agent in your book, the next line of attack is to contact book publishers directly.

Unfortunately, a number of major publishers will not accept unsolicited manuscripts (manuscripts sent without prior request). Among the major publishers that will not accept unsolicited manuscripts are McGraw-Hill, Simon & Schuster, G. P. Putnam's, William Morrow, Bantam, Dell and Doubleday.

The largest of the trade book publishers, Doubleday & Company, has prepared a letter that is sent to "first authors" telling them how to submit their book idea to Doubleday. Because the letter is so clear and helpful for any prospective author, it is reprinted in its entirety in the Appendix.

All of the major book publishers are listed in the *LMP*. In addition to their addresses and phone numbers, the names of most of the major editors at each of the publishing firms are also listed and it is a good idea when you are submitting your book to a publisher to route your letter, phone call or manuscript to a specific editor. I would strongly suggest that you not select the editor-in-chief since he or she is usually overwhelmed by manuscripts. Choose one of the other editors listed in the *LMP*.

If you are determined to submit a manuscript to a publishing firm that does not accept unsolicited manuscripts, then your best approach is to first try to contact one of the editors over the phone to see if he or she would be interested in looking at your book proposal. If the answer is affirmative, then obviously your manuscript no longer falls into the category of unsolicited manuscript. You can then send it directly to that editor.

If your manuscript is being represented by a literary agent or if you are dealing directly with a publisher, you must develop a degree of patience. Book publishing does not provide instant gratification. Only on the rarest of occasions does a publisher contract for a book immediately after receiving the outline, sample chapter or the completed manuscript. It takes time. With major book publishers it usually takes a minimum of three weeks, often longer.

The reason for the delay is that the decision to buy a book and publish it is not made by one person at a publishing firm but rather by a number of people and in the case of some publishing firms, by an editorial board.

Let's assume that your book has been accepted by a publisher and he wants to offer you a contract. How do you make money as an author and what are the things you should know?

If you are represented by a literary agent, the agent will obviously guide you through the process of contract negotiation and act on your behalf.

If you are not using a literary agent, you should by all means have an attorney who is familiar with book publishing contracts read over any contract before you sign it.

Every book publisher has a standard contract that is subject to negotiation. The willingness of the publisher to change the standard contract will depend on the strength of their desire to publish your book. The more they want your manuscript, the more they will be willing to bend and change certain clauses in the contract in your favor.

As a general rule, a publisher pays an advance and a royalty to every author whose book he publishes.

The advance payment is the amount of money that the publisher is willing to risk for the author to write the book. The advance payment can be as little as $1,000 or as much as $1,000,000 or more. Obviously the major advance payments go to established authors or to authors whose books look like natural bestsellers.

In negotiating this advance payment, if you don't have an agent, you will be representing yourself; and the truth is that for a first book you will be wise to accept whatever advance the publisher offers unless, of course, it is so low that it doesn't make it worthwhile to write the book.

You should bear in mind, however, that where you really make money in book publishing is on the royalties. The royalty is based on every copy sold by the book publisher.

In the case of hardcover books, the royalty you receive is usually between 10% and 15% depending on the number of copies sold. Most of the publishers offer a royalty of 10% on copies sold up to and including 5,000 copies; 12½% on copies sold over and above 5,000 copies up to and including 10,000 copies; and 15% on copies sold thereafter. There has been a trend lately by many publishers to offer a straight royalty of 10% because of the high cost of producing books.

Your royalty (in most instances) is based on the selling price of the book. In other words, if your royalty is 15% and your book sells for $10, you will be earning $1.50 on every copy sold.

The key word here is *sold* because when a publisher sells a book to a bookstore, it is literally on consignment. Most unsold books are fully returnable. A publisher may distribute 50,000 copies of your book through bookstores but only 20,000 may eventually be sold. That is why book publishers issue royalty statements only twice a year so that the royalty statement can best reflect the copies sold—not just to the bookstores but to the actual book buyer.

In addition, before you can realize any royalties on a book that is published, you must earn back your advance payment. If, for instance, your advance payment was $5,000, then before you receive any additional monies, you would have to earn back the $5,000 advance out of the royalties. Once your royalty payments exceed $5,000, you will, of course, receive the additional monies.

Aside from the advance payment and the royalties, there are other ways that you can make money as an author. They include first serial sales (an excerpt from your book is sold to a magazine prior to publication) or second serial sales (an excerpt from your book is sold to a magazine after publication).

You can also earn additional money from paperback sales, foreign sales and book clubs. In the case of paperback sales, second serial sales and book clubs, you usually share income with the publisher on a fifty-fifty basis.

In the case of first serial and foreign sales, the split between you and the publisher depends in many instances on whether you have an agent. Usually, agents represent you for first serial, foreign and motion picture and television sales.

I have so far, I hope, clearly explained the process of how to secure a publisher and how the financial arrangements are determined in book publishing.

Now here is the most important question of all: Should you be an author?

I have to admit that I am an evangelist in this area and that I believe that the opportunities in book publishing are limitless. I believe that the story of Francine Prince can be, and is, repeated in book publishing every day.

You don't have to be a Norman Mailer or a James Michener to succeed in book publishing. You need a good idea well executed and, of course, some luck.

In my own case, more than twenty years ago I thought there was a book in the humorous and touching letters that kids write from camp. I had attended summer camp as a camper and a counselor and I knew that the letters and postcards that kids mailed to their relatives and friends from camp were often delightfully funny.

Once I got the idea for *Letters from Camp,* I contacted my friends who had children at camps and asked them to save their letters. I collected about 125 of the funniest letters and through determination secured the services of one of the largest literary agencies, the Scott

Meredith Agency, which sold the book for an advance of $2,000 to Chilton Publishing Company in Philadelphia.

Since its original publication more than twenty years ago, *Letters from Camp* has sold more than 1,000,000 copies in all editions and we easily financed the college education of our children from the monies earned from that book.

But how do you find an idea for your own book if you don't already have one? The best answer is that probably the idea for *your* book is so obvious that you have overlooked it. It could be a particular expertise that you have in a specific area or something out of your professional background or an experience that you have had that would be of interest to others.

The best category for your first book is nonfiction. To be brutally frank, the standards for execution of the manuscript and writing skills in nonfiction are not as demanding as they are in fiction. There are not specific statistics on this, but it is axiomatic in book publishing that the chances for a first nonfiction book to succeed are much greater than for a first novel.

If, however, you are determined to write a novel and you feel that your talents lie in that area, you certainly should proceed. Although fiction is the most treacherous area in book publishing for both publisher and author, there have been many instances where first novels have been a bonanza for both the publisher and the new novelist.

After all, Judith Krantz had never written a novel before the success of *Scruples* only a few years ago. And it wasn't long ago that Stephen King was just an unpublished author; then Doubleday decided to publish his first novel, *Carrie.*

Only recently, Anne Tolstoi Wallach, author of *Women's Work,* was working as a vice president at the Grey advertising agency where she is still employed. Now her first novel is a main selection of the Literary Guild, and a full selection of the Doubleday Book Club, and her total advance payments prior to publication were $850,000.

Incidentally, in the case of Anne Tolstoi Wallach's novel *Women's Work,* the setting is the advertising business—obviously an industry she knows something about.

It is always sound advice to write your first novel about an area that you are familiar with. The opportunities are greater for the novel if it has a ring of authenticity.

The best place to begin your research for a book idea is in a bookstore. As an author, I have developed more than fifty books that have been published. Many of those came about because I spent time in bookstores observing what had been published and, most important, what had not been published. Often a trip to a bookstore will stimulate an idea that can make you money.

Other good sources for book ideas are obviously magazines and newspapers.

In 1961, I read an article in the old *Saturday Evening Post* about President John Kennedy. In the article the author gave some examples of Kennedy's dry humor and wit. It was only a few paragraphs in the overall story in the *Saturday Evening Post*, but those few paragraphs gave me the idea for a book that was eventually published titled *The Kennedy Wit*.

The advance payment for *The Kennedy Wit* was only $2,500 and more than thirty-five publishers turned the book down before Citadel Press agreed to publish it.

The Kennedy Wit was a national bestseller and was on the *New York Times* Best Sellers list for six months and sold more than 100,000 copies in hardcover alone. I earned more than $75,000 on *The Kennedy Wit*—and all of that as a result of reading a few paragraphs in an article in a magazine.

There are book ideas everywhere—in your home, in bookstores, in magazine articles, in newspapers, in television interviews. If you want to write a book, the chances are good you will find an idea.

Obviously, in order to write a book you must be able to write English competently, but your literary skills are not as important in nonfiction as the strength of the idea and your determination to get it published.

That's the good news. The bad news is that if you are thinking of making writing your only livelihood, you should be aware of these rather frightening statistics.

According to a study released by the Columbia University Center for Social Sciences, the average book author's income from writing is $4,775 a year.

Only recently *Publishers Weekly*, the trade publication for the book industry, carried a long article titled "Can Writers Afford to Write Books?" The article and the overall survey of 2,239 published book writers revealed the following startling statistics:

> Only 5 percent of all the writers who are published authors are able to take care of their needs over any extended length of time.
>
> Only 38 percent of the full-time writers in America earn more than $20,000 a year.

For the beginner, therefore, writing should be an avocation, not a full-time occupation.

Writing can be stimulating, exciting and potentially profitable, but the chances for real success are obviously hard to come by.

How to Make a Sale

ANYONE who sells books to publishers (agents, authors or anyone else) has his or her own philosophy on the best way to find a publisher for a book property.

There are many agents who like to submit book properties to a number of publishers at the same time—like the book auction, this is called "multiple submission."

The difference between a book auction and a multiple submission is that in a multiple submission the agent does not necessarily let the publishers know other publishers are considering the book at the same time, and there is not necessarily a deadline by which the publisher must reply.

There is a growing trend among literary agents to submit virtually everything to publishers via the technique of multiple submissions. The reason for this is that so many publishers take so long to respond to a book proposal that if you went from publisher to publisher you might spend two years finding a publisher who would be willing to buy the book property and make an offer.

With multiple submissions (five to ten publishers at the same time), you can find out rather quickly if you are going to make a sale, and it helps to soothe the impatience of the anxious author you are representing.

Many agents, however, and others who are selling book properties to publishers, prefer to deal publisher by publisher on a one-to-one basis. If they have a book property that they feel is just right for Random House, they will begin with Random House rather than submit the book proposal on a multiple basis.

There are advantages to both ways of selling a book property as there are obviously advantages to auctioning off a book when you feel that the book auction will best serve your client.

I have no favorite technique for selling a book except for an underlying philosophy that I believe works more often than not. That philosophy isn't complicated and it can be best described as the "quick kill."

One of my favorite lines to an author or anyone else I represent who prefers to drag out the selling process in search of the best possible deal is to simply state that "with the rate of inflation increasing and the value of the dollar decreasing almost daily, the longer you wait the less you are going to get anyway in terms of real buying power." You are better off accepting $20,000 for a book in January than you are in accepting $21,000 four months later. In the four months that have passed, you will not only get greater value for that $20,000 but, most important, you will have had the use of the money.

That does not mean, of course, that I don't believe in getting the best deal for my books or in utilizing multiple submissions or auctions. It is my contention, though, that if you have a reasonable and a fair offer for a book property you should accept it as quickly as you can, not only because of the diminishing value of the dollar but because you may discover that someone else has announced a book on the very same subject or close to it—therefore effectively killing your book property.

As a matter of fact as I write this, I have a major book property scheduled for publication very soon, and we have just discovered that another publisher has a book on the same subject by an equally qualified author coming out at the same time as the book we represent. Few enough people in this country buy books, and if there are to be two books on the same subject at the same time, it will be detrimental to both.

Not only do I believe in selling a book as quickly as possible but I am equally aggressive in pressing the publisher for the contract once the deal has been set as well as pressing for any payments due the author upon signing of the contract. Lately, many publishers have been notoriously slow in drafting contracts and even slower in making the payments.

On more than one occasion a book has actually been finished before we received the contract and long before the author received his advance payment. Although most companies won't admit to it, the truth is that the publishers are also trying to get the maximum use out of their money and therefore in many cases are dragging out the contract and, certainly, the payment process.

I won't name the publishers because perhaps the situation will change, but the fact is that at least half a dozen of the major book publishers are taking at least twice as long as they used to take to pay advances to authors upon signing of contracts and completion of manuscripts.

There is another reason to press a publisher for a book contract as soon as you have made the deal. In an industry where musical chairs among editors has become more prevalent of late as editors frequently jump from one publishing house to another, it is not unusual to sell a book to an editor one month and then discover the following month that the editor has moved on to another publishing house. You have to pray in that case that the new editor assigned to the book will feel the same way about it as the original editor.

Not only do the editors come and go at publishing firms but of late, editors-in-chief, marketing directors and publishers themselves have been moving from one house to another with such speed that the Rolodex in our office looks as if the entire publishing industry is in transit. As a matter of fact, the *LMP* is virtually out-of-date by the time it is published.

Taking all the factors into consideration, I am absolutely convinced that, on balance, the best deal is a quick deal and that if a book is really going to make money, it will make it in the market place where the buying public has the final word on whether a book has it or doesn't.

One of the most interesting trends that has taken place in book publishing in the last few years is that more and more books are being sold without outlines or written presentations. This is especially true of big book properties. In the last six months we have sold at least ten books for advances of over $50,000 where the presentation to the publisher by me acting as agent was either just a phone call or a face-to-face meeting. In most of these instances the decision to buy the book was made quickly—sometimes within the space of ten minutes.

One recent incident perhaps best illustrates the point. I had a meeting with the president of a major publishing firm to discuss two book properties. I presented the idea verbally for the first book and the president said, "How much?" I quickly replied "$250,000" and the publisher said, "It's a deal."

Even though it was only a quick verbal presentation and a description of the book, the response was immediate and affirmative from the publisher.

I then made another verbal presentation of the idea for the second book I had come to discuss. The president listened to my five-minute presentation without comment and then asked, "How much do you want for that book?" My reply was an equally fast, "$7,500." The publisher thought for a moment and then said, "I think I would like to see an outline for that book."

The story is true and, of course, I'm not going to reveal who the president of the publishing firm was, but I do think he made the wise decision in both cases. The real point of the story is that publishers today are willing to buy expensive books quickly with little presentation except a few words for fear that someone else will grab the book before they do. The competition among publishers for what are called in the industry "major properties" is fierce. It is the smaller books that are harder to sell and in many instances require outlines or substantial written presentations. It is easier today to sell a book for one million dollars than it is for ten thousand.

Mood swings are important in selling a book successfully to a publisher—not necessarily your mood but the mood of the individual you are trying to sell to at the publishing firm. I, for example, hardly ever try to sell a book at five o'clock in the afternoon. By that time, most people are too tired, too tense and too exasperated. I prefer to do most of my selling in the morning—before lunch—when the trials of the day have not taken their toll. I have, however, sold books to publishers at breakfast, lunch, over a cocktail and even while riding in an elevator or walking along Madison Avenue.

I remember a particular incident with the president of a publishing firm who has since retired. We were walking along the streets of Manhattan on our way to our respective homes. For the first four blocks, I described the idea for the book I was trying to interest him in. By the time we had reached the sixth block, he liked the idea and three blocks later we had made a deal.

I like to close a deal quickly and not give the buyer too much time to reconsider the proposition. If I am pitching a book to a publisher and I have a figure of $20,000 in my head and the publisher only offers $18,000, I will probably take the $18,000 on the spot rather than have him say something to the effect that he would like to think it over at $20,000. I once presented a book to a publisher and I really thought I should get $25,000 for the property. The publisher was enthusiastic and said he wanted to do the book. However, he felt that the best he could offer was $22,500. When I told him that I needed $25,000 for this property, he said he wanted to think about it overnight and discuss it with his associates. I knew I was dead.

Sure enough, the next day the publisher called to say that he had thought about it and discussed it with some of the editors and had decided not to take on the book. At that point, the publisher wasn't interested in the property at $25,000, $22,500 or, for that matter, at any price at all. I don't make that mistake often. I have learned from experience that if too many people are involved in the discussion of the buying of a book property or if too much time elapses, people can change their minds, and what could have been an easy sale turns out to be no sale at all.

Richard Snyder, the brilliant president of Simon & Schuster, is a publisher who will on occasion make a fast decision when he feels it is justified. One evening a few years ago, Snyder and I were having a drink at the King Cole bar at the St. Regis Hotel. I proposed a book. There was nothing in writing and the entire presentation was verbal. It didn't take very long because the value of the property was obvious—at least to Richard Snyder. Dick's immediate response was that he wanted to publish the book and then his next question was "How much?" I replied, "$100,000." "It's a deal," Dick said and we went on to discuss other matters and never again referred to the $100,000 deal we had made. Two weeks later, I received the contract for the book from Simon & Schuster, and not only did I make my $10,000 commission in that brief sale but Dick even paid for the drinks.

There is, of course, the possibility that the property Dick bought from me at the St. Regis might have been worth $150,000 or $200,000 but the flip side of that is that the property might have been worth only $50,000. By settling on a figure of $100,000 quickly, both buyer and seller made a deal without agonizing or prolonged discussions and negotiations.

There are some publishers who get in very early in the morning before the switchboards open and before their staffs arrive. Lawrence Hughes, the president of William Morrow & Co., gets in very early. Jack Artenstein, the president of the trade paperback and juvenile publishing division at Simon & Schuster, is an early man (very early). Harold Roth, when he was president of Grosset & Dunlap, was also in his office before anyone else; and Michael Korda, editor-in-chief at Simon & Schuster, is one of the earliest arrivals. Phyllis Grann, the publisher of G. P. Putnam's, is at her desk before nine and there are others who also have the early habit.

I try to do business with the executives who get in early before their switchboards open. It requires that you have their direct line numbers (which I do) and the advantage, of course, is that you can talk to them about books before they are preoccupied with the normal and abnormal problems of the business day. On more than one morning, I make two book deals before nine o'clock rolls around.

If you are trying to sell a book and you are a literary agent, the worst time is lunchtime. With some minor exceptions, virtually no one in book publishing is at his desk during lunch, so unless you are taking a publisher to lunch there is little you can do to sell a book from noon until half-past two.

If you are going to sell a book it is important to know how the various publishing firms buy books. I don't intend to discuss how every publishing house buys a book, but I think it will be worthwhile to talk about some of the major companies and how they decide whether to buy a book or not.

Simon & Schuster operates through an editorial board that meets for lunch every Thursday in the company dining room. If you want to sell a book to Simon & Schuster, you first submit the book to one of their editors who, of course, has the option of rejecting it. If, however, the editor to whom you have submitted the book would like to have the book considered for publication, then the editor must circulate the manuscript or proposal to the members of the editorial board which is composed of senior editors including, among others, Richard Snyder and Michael Korda. It is at these editorial board luncheons that decisions are made as to whether to buy or reject a book. The editorial board even determines how much money should be offered for the book property. At approximately half-past two when the editorial board lunch is over various members of the board notify the editors who in turn notify the agents and authors.

Simon & Schuster can, of course, buy books in other ways such as through direct contact with the president of the company, Richard Snyder. In the fast-paced publishing world of today decisions sometimes cannot wait until editorial boards meet, so Snyder has to act without waiting for the board. But, in general, Simon & Schuster operates through their Thursday luncheon meetings.

If you are dealing with a small publishing firm like M. Evans, the selling process is a little less complicated. Herbert Katz who is the editor-in-chief at M. Evans is accessible to agents and authors and if Katz wants to buy a book it isn't necessary for him to discuss it with an editorial board. He can make the decision himself after perhaps discussing it with one or two editors or marketing people.

That is one of the advantages of dealing with a small publishing firm where the editor-in-chief is the principal decision maker in the company and therefore answers come quickly. The same is true if you are selling a book to Rawson Associates and you are dealing with Eleanor or Ken Rawson. Again, you are talking to the principals of the firm and the decision can come without a lot of corporate paper work.

On the other hand, if you are proposing a book to Doubleday (the largest trade publisher in the country), the route is a lot more complicated. A book that is submitted to an editor at Doubleday must go through the committees at Doubleday which include their publishing and marketing boards. The process can take a long time and although the company can act quickly if pressed, my experience has been that Doubleday does not respond as readily as some of the smaller publishing firms in deciding whether to buy a book or not.

An easy firm to deal with when submitting a book property is William Morrow, one of the largest publishing houses. At Morrow a book is submitted to an editor who then discusses it with Hillel Black, the editor-in-chief, or presents the book directly to the president, Lawrence Hughes. It is Larry Hughes who makes the final decision after consulting with his editor and sales and marketing people. Since there are only one or two people involved in the book buying process at William Morrow, they can, and often do, respond speedily. Morrow is certainly faster than Doubleday and can be faster than Simon & Schuster because they don't have an editorial board.

I have always found Larry Hughes to be a publisher with excellent judgment when it comes to buying books.

Before Dan Rather became the star that he is today, I proposed a book to Larry Hughes and Hillel Black who was then a senior editor. The book was titled *The Camera Never Blinks* by Dan Rather and Mickey Herskowitz. At the time Rather had just left his assignment as CBS White House correspondent and his future was slightly uncertain. Larry and Hillel were not interested in the book at any price. I could have taken the book property to another publisher but it was my intuitive feeling that Morrow would be the best publisher for Dan Rather. I waited a day or two and then I went back to discuss the book again with Larry and Hillel. This time my argument for publishing Dan Rather centered around my own judgment. I told Larry and Hillel that I was absolutely convinced Dan Rather was going to be an important personality and that his book would be a bestseller. I also told them that I could certainly present the book to someone else and I was confident I would make a sale but that I wanted Morrow to publish the book. Three minutes later Larry Hughes and Hillel Black agreed to publish *The Camera Never Blinks* by Dan Rather and Mickey Herskowitz and we went from no offer at all to an advance of $40,000, a healthy one at the time.

The Camera Never Blinks went on to become a bestseller and was on the *New York Times* list for more than six months.

At other major publishing firms such as Random House, Bantam, Putnam's, McGraw-Hill, Macmillan, Holt and Little, Brown, the process for buying a book is usually through an editor who then consults with his editor-in-chief or the publisher of the company. The speed with which a publishing firm buys a book depends in large part on the ability of the editor to maneuver within the buying process and the clout that he or she has within the publishing firm.

A good agent should be aware of which editors at which houses lean toward certain kinds of books. If you are going to sell a celebrity book, then an excellent publishing firm would be Simon & Schuster, Dell or Morrow. All three have had great success with books by and about celebrities.

If you are trying to sell a diet book, it would be wise to offer that book to Rawson Associates (which published *The Scarsdale Diet*), to Macmillan (which published *The Beverly Hills Diet*), to Morrow (which published Dr. Atkins's diet book) or to any other publisher that has been successful with diet books.

It is important in selling a book to a prospective publisher that you have a sense of their track record in various categories of publishing. Phyllis Grann of Putnam's has been enormously successful with fiction so if you are selling a novel, Phyllis would be a good person to talk to.

Most publishing firms are interested in all kinds of books—fiction and nonfiction—but the best approach is still to offer publishing firms books in areas in which they have had past success. They obviously understand the potential of the book better than a publishing firm that has had no successful track record in that particular area.

The same is true of editors. There are editors who are superb at self-help books or novels or books of an historical or a political nature. It takes awhile to learn who they are and what they are interested in but once you do, it makes your sales job easier and more effective.

On more than one occasion when talking to a prospective publisher, I have heard the statement, "We don't know how to handle that kind of book." Frankly, I have always thought that a silly response since a publisher should be able to market any kind of book. But the reality is that each publisher seems to have carved out a particular niche for itself and you will frequently hear comments within the industry like, "that's a Simon & Schuster book" or "that book is perfect for Morrow" or "Doubleday would really know how to handle that book."

There are specialized publishers who are superb with certain kinds of books. Workman Publishing Co. is one of the best for what can be best described as the "nonbook" book. Workman's most recent smashing success in the nonbook book category is *The Official Preppy Handbook.* Prior to that, Workman came out with *"cat"* by Kliban which was one of the most successful "cat" books of all time. Workman not only promotes with great imagination in the nonbook category but they are, I think, one of the best publishers around.

There are other publishers uniquely qualified for certain types of books. Crown Publishers is very good with nonfiction books ranging from antiques to collecting stamps, and recently Crown has broken through in the fiction area with *Scruples* and *The Spike.*

Crown publishes a lot of books and, although I have never felt they paid the highest advances in publishing, they certainly do turn out a lot of product, much of which has been enormously successful. Crown is one of the largest publishers not owned by a conglomerate or another corporation. The guiding genius behind Crown is Nat Wartels who is a contemporary legend in book publishing.

For a number of years, Coward, McCann and Viking Press have been two of the largest publishers of sports books. The sales staff at both publishing houses know how to market a sports book and have had an enormous amount of experience in that area.

One of the tricks of the trade that I have developed over the years in selling books to publishers is that it is sometimes much easier to sell to an editor who has just joined a firm. New editors are usually given a chance to bring in books and prove themselves, and if you happen to submit a book to an editor who is in the first six months of stewardship, your chances of making a sale are greatly improved. The same is also true if the leadership of a house changes hands. The new executives are anxious to put their stamp on the company with their own books.

Perhaps the worst time to try to sell a book is when publishers are preparing for their sales conferences, which usually take place twice a year. Editors are very busy and preoccupied the week before sales conferences preparing the materials they are going to present to the salesmen, and it is not the most auspicious time to talk about new books.

Publishing sales conferences usually last for about a week and, as I indicated earlier, they are held twice a year since most publishers have two major selling periods in which they sell books to the bookstores.

One of the serious problems in book publishing is the length of time it takes for a publisher to get a manuscript once a book has been signed up. Books can take anywhere from six months to one year to two years and beyond to be written. Occasionally you can seal a book deal if one of your selling points is the ability to deliver the manuscript within a shorter space of time.

Just recently we sold three nonfiction books to a publisher who was interested in the books but equally excited about the fact that the manuscript for each of the books would be delivered within forty-five days. The publisher desperately needed some product for the next list and our ability to have the manuscripts delivered quickly was a major factor in their decision to move forward.

Flights of Fancy

or Books I Would Give Anything to Represent

EVERY author, agent, publisher or, for that matter, anyone else intimately connected with book publishing has a special list of books that he would like to represent and publish. I, too, have such a list.

Frequently, when I appear on radio or television or give lectures on book publishing, I am asked the same question: "If you could represent any five books in the world as a literary agent, which five would they be and why?"

Obviously, the questioners are asking about books that have never been written or published for even if I have wanted to represent Winston Churchill's *The Gathering Storm* or Tolstoy's *War and Peace,* those books have already been spoken for.

Therefore, not in any particular order, I would like to present my candidates for the five books that I believe would be enormous best-sellers and which I would certainly like to represent.

In presenting these five books, I have to make two basic assumptions. First and foremost is that they will be written well and honestly. The second assumption is that the publishers will recognize the enormous potential of the books and publicize them accordingly.

I am only going to deal with nonfiction because it is almost impossible to discuss novels that you would like to represent since novels are usually not "created" or developed as in the case of nonfiction properties.

I would give anything to represent Pat Nixon's autobiography, especially if she dealt honestly and frankly with the joys, trials and tribulations of her life with Richard M. Nixon.

I remember recently watching Mike Wallace being asked on a television program who among those he has not interviewed he would like most to talk to. Wallace replied, "Pat Nixon." While I don't have any particular desire to interview Pat Nixon (especially since that is not my business), I certainly consider her to be one of the major book properties as yet unpublished. People identify with Mrs. Nixon and they feel for what she has been through. Pat Nixon came through the Watergate episode as a courageous figure and if there were ever a book that would appeal to women, it would be hers. It is my judgment that Pat Nixon's story could be one of the major bestsellers of all time.

The Kennedys have always been important book properties. John F. Kennedy's own book, *Profiles in Courage,* was a bestseller and books about the Kennedys have always done well in the market place. In the early sixties I edited a little book titled *The Kennedy Wit* which was on the *New York Times* Best Sellers list for more than six months. There is no question that the Kennedys have been and are American royalty and during the years when John F. Kennedy was president—and since—there have certainly been more books written about that period than almost any other subject in American history with the possible exception of Abraham Lincoln.

There are three Kennedy books which, if written, would be enormous bestsellers and I am including all three as a group.

Those three books, of course, would be Edward M. Kennedy's autobiography, Jacqueline Kennedy Onassis's autobiography and Ethel Kennedy's autobiography. Each in his or her own way has a fascinating story to tell.

Ted Kennedy because of his close relationship with his two brothers and his own public tragedy at Chappaquiddick, which he has never dealt with in print. Also Senator Kennedy writing about growing up as a Kennedy is a story worth telling.

Ethel Kennedy's story is one of personal courage. She is a positive figure with strong qualities and an inner strength which would make her book one that would appeal to both men and women. Mrs. Robert Kennedy's life as a widow raising her eleven children is a story that would touch people around the world.

The one Kennedy book that would have the strongest sale would be, of course, the one written by Jacqueline Kennedy Onassis. Mrs. Onassis is currently working as an editor at Doubleday, and I would assume that if she ever decided to write her book while she was working at Doubleday they would have the first opportunity to publish it.

I don't think it's necessary to elaborate on the reasons why Mrs. Onassis's book would be so successful since Jacqueline Kennedy Onassis is probably the most famous woman in the world and there isn't a country anywhere on earth where her book would not become an immediate bestseller. I don't think it is an overstatement to say that never before has there been a woman who has had the wide appeal and notoriety of Jacqueline Kennedy Onassis. Any agent would give up virtually all his authors to represent that one book and any publisher would offer Mrs. Onassis a blank check to acquire her story.

For years within the book industry, there has been talk about Frank Sinatra writing his autobiography but he has not done so. Sometime perhaps, Frank Sinatra will write his own story and I must include that book on my list. Of all the entertainers performing today, Sinatra is one of the best known. But what's more important is that his life has been fascinating and he has had more than his share of crises and triumphs. Sinatra is a legendary figure not only in his own country but wherever people listen to music.

Sinatra has been the subject of much innuendo and rumor during his exciting lifetime and if he would deal with those stories openly, the book would be one of the best book properties of all time.

Because somebody is famous or well-known doesn't necessarily mean that his book will be an instantaneous success, but in the case of the Kennedys, Pat Nixon and Sinatra, their stories are so dramatic and so intriguing and their lives have prompted so much speculation that they fall into a category of book properties that is very special.

The next name that would go on my list of book properties that I would like to represent is Cary Grant. Perhaps some people in the industry would want to include Greta Garbo rather than Cary Grant, but it is my feeling that Cary Grant is a much more fascinating book property. First of all, Cary Grant has been continuously in the public eye longer than Greta Garbo and he has been one of the real major film stars of our time. Grant's numerous marriages and his turbulent personal life make him as fascinating off the screen as he is on.

There are very few stars left today of the caliber of Cary Grant who have not written autobiographies. Sophia Loren has written her story, Ingrid Bergman hers, as have Lauren Bacall, Doris Day and, most recently, Henry Fonda. James Stewart is currently working on his autobiography and Burt Reynolds has signed a contract with Hearst (Arbor House in hardcover and Avon in paperback) to write his autobiography. Just as an aside, Burt Reynolds, I understand, received $1,000,000 for the hard and softcover rights to his autobiography and if Burt Reynolds's story is worth one million, then Cary Grant's story is worth at least twice that.

Cary Grant has worldwide appeal and since the foreign market for books can be more important than the American market, Grant's story would be published and be a bestseller everywhere in the world.

There are other names I would want to put on this list. One would be the personal story of Yoko Ono. Yoko Ono is not as famous as Pat Nixon, the Kennedys, Sinatra or Cary Grant but because she was the wife of John Lennon who died so tragically, her story would capture the imagination of millions of people. The Beatles were, of course, a phenomenon of our time, and I doubt if any group of singers or performers will ever again capture the world's fancy as they did.

Yoko Ono was not only married to John Lennon but she was intimately involved in his professional career as well. They wrote music together and collaborated on songs. Yoko Ono would not only be able to write about her personal life with John Lennon but would be able to write about the other Beatles.

There are other subjects for autobiographies that I believe would have the opportunity to be bestsellers around the world and, although I am not convinced that they would necessarily be as successful as the books I have mentioned, I think they would be enormously successful.

Those books would include Priscilla Presley's story about her life with Elvis; Joe DiMaggio's autobiography, especially if he would write candidly about his marriage to Marilyn Monroe; Mrs. Clark Gable writing about her marriage; Grace Kelly's story which would be an international bestseller because she is the fairy princess of all time.

If Rudolph Hess were well enough to write a book about his life and the Third Reich, that would not only be a bestseller but would be an important document for better understanding that tragic period of world history.

I have always believed that Johnny Carson's autobiography would be an extremely popular book and would be bought by the millions of people who are fascinated by one of the finest entertainers of our time. Carson's life story is a complex one, and I believe it would be a major book property.

Henry Ford should write a book about his family—his father, his grandfather—because there have been few American industrial families as important or fascinating as the Fords.

I would love to represent Happy Rockefeller writing about her life with Nelson Rockefeller—another legendary figure with a name that is known around the world.

Lucille Ball certainly should write her book because the "Lucy" television programs have been shown around the world thousands and thousands of times. Her book would be an international bestseller.

Emperor Hirohito of Japan should write his story, and if he did it with candor and honesty, especially in relation to World War II, it would be one of the more important books of our time.

General Douglas MacArthur has been the subject of many books including William Manchester's recent penetrating biography, *American Caesar: Douglas MacArthur,* but no book about the general—what he was like, what he believed, what he thought and how he felt—would be as important as the book by his widow. If Mrs. MacArthur would write about her life with one of the most famous generals in American history, it would be a major book with worldwide appeal.

If she steps down from the throne, Queen Elizabeth of England should write her memoirs. To my knowledge this has never been done by any English monarch.

It goes without saying that if Elizabeth Taylor were to write her autobiography, it would be an instantaneous bestseller. Not only is Elizabeth Taylor a legendary movie star but her life in many ways reads like a soap opera—with tragedies and triumphs galore. Elizabeth Taylor is such a good book property that a recent book about her by Kitty Kelley published by Simon & Schuster earned over one million dollars in subsidiary rights for the author before publication. You can easily imagine what the "real McCoy" would be worth.

It is obvious from the names on this list that I believe that personal stories or autobiographies or stories about relationships with other people are an important category in book publishing.

Hundreds of books have been written about World War II but only when the participants in the events write about them do they have real meaning and truth. That is why a book by Rudolph Hess and the personal recollections of Mrs. Douglas MacArthur would be so significant.

The really great books and the ones that really sell are not written secondhand but rather on a personal basis by those who have lived the stories they are writing about.

4

Image and Reality

I have always believed that one of the keys to success in any business or, for that matter, to life in general relates largely to perception. The axiom that I believe sums it all up is "You are as you are perceived." How people perceive you is hard to shake and this is not only true in business relationships but equally true in virtually every aspect of life.

Jimmy Carter, Richard Nixon, Adolf Hitler, Winston Churchill, Franklin D. Roosevelt, John F. Kennedy and Ronald Reagan are perceived in a certain way—people have an image of them, a preconceived notion of what they were or are like and how they think.

The same is true in book publishing. There are certain individuals and certain publishing firms whose public image may or may not be accurate but exists nevertheless.

I know that I have a reputation in the industry and that I am perceived in a certain manner by publishers, editors and other agents. In many instances, that perception might be true but the reality of what we are does not always relate to the perception others have of us. Image is almost as important as reality and many people in book publishing have succeeded or failed because of their image—not because of what they really were or really did.

All of this is by way of introduction to some of the more exciting characters in book publishing and to present them as they are seen by others but not necessarily as they really are.

Like any other industry, book publishing has its share of gossip and cocktail party rumors and much of what we think of our colleagues is a result of what we hear at lunches, dinners or over a drink at the Four Seasons.

Probably the one person in book publishing in the last four or five years who has received the most publicity and press coverage and is therefore perceived in a certain manner as a result of that coverage is Richard E. Snyder, the president of Simon & Schuster.

Dick Snyder's life story is very much like the American dream. He grew up in Brooklyn in a middle-class family. He joined the sales department at Simon & Schuster, became sales manager with a seat on the editorial board and then was given complete charge of all fiscal commitments made by Simon & Schuster. When Leon Shimkin became chairman of the board, Dick Snyder was named president of Simon & Schuster. Today Snyder is chairman of the board, president and chief executive officer.

Richard Snyder leads what is perhaps the most exciting and dynamic of the publishing firms. Simon & Schuster has sales well in excess of $100 million a year. The highly articulate Snyder is perceived as a demanding man to work for and one who wants 100 percent effort from his people. But he is also perceived as an honest man who says what he thinks and is willing to go to court to defend the rights of his publishing firm.

Within the publishing industry Snyder is considered to be more of a gambler than most publishers, someone who has a sense for the market and is especially tuned in to the book possibilities of celebrities and media personalities.

There are very few publishing executives who understand the phenomenon and impact of media personalities as well as Snyder. He is quick to grasp the potential of a media personality for a book, and when I represented Phil Donahue's autobiography, Dick Snyder bought it immediately without any hesitation. This, of course, turned out to be one of the best publishing decisions Snyder has ever made since the paperback rights alone for Donahue's book were sold to Fawcett for over $1,600,000.

As long as he is active in the publishing industry, Snyder will be perceived as a hard driving, creative, no-nonsense publisher.

At Simon & Schuster there is another personality who is perceived within the industry in a particular manner which may or may not be fair or accurate. That individual is Michael Korda, the vice president and editor-in-chief of Simon & Schuster, who has probably received more publicity and exposure than any other editor today.

Michael Korda is considered to be a superb acquisitions editor and when all is said and done what most houses are interested in more than anything is someone who can acquire top properties successfully and beat out the competition when it comes to getting the big books and the books that really sell.

It isn't easy to be a first-rate acquisitions editor. The requirements are tough. You have to circulate constantly among the top agents and be friendly with agents that really count like Swifty Lazar, Morton Janklow, Owen Laster and Scott Meredith. For every autobiography by Henry Fonda or Shelley Winters or Lauren Bacall or a new novel by Ken Follett, Judith Krantz or Robert Ludlum, there are thirty publishers who would like to publish the book. And those publishers compete where it counts—with their checkbooks.

The great acquisitions editors not only are close to the agents who represent the major book properties but they travel in a circle where the celebrities gather so that when Lauren Bacall or Doris Day or some other personality of major worth is thinking of writing a book the names of the top editors are already known to them.

Michael Korda is an editor whose name comes to mind quite often. He has been a visible editor primarily because he has written a number of books himself, including his first national bestseller, *Power: How to Get It, How to Use It,* and his latest bestselling book, *Charmed Lives.* Because he is a successful author, Korda has appeared on all the national television shows including, of course, "Today" and the "Donahue" show. Korda is a celebrity in his own right and celebrities feel comfortable working with each other, which is why Michael Korda edits so many of the celebrity books published by Simon & Schuster.

Some of the celebrity books he has edited are Phil Donahue's autobiography, Kitty Kelley's *Elizabeth Taylor: The Last Star,* Garson Kanin's *Movieola,* John Houseman's *On Stage,* Cheryl Tiegs's *Beauty Book* and Jacqueline Susann's *The Love Machine.*

Korda is known as a brilliant line editor who works quickly and who understands how to shape a manuscript. Only recently, Irving Mansfield, Jacqueline Susann's husband and the well-known television producer, told me of his experiences with Michael Korda when Korda edited Jacqueline Susann's *Once Is Not Enough*, which went on to be the number one bestseller in the country. As Mansfield told the story, there were at least fifteen or twenty pages in the original manuscript that related to a political convention. Korda felt that those pages really got in the way of the story and he gently but firmly told the author that he believed that the best way to handle the description of the convention was to simply have two lines saying something to the effect that "the Democratic convention was held."

Jacqueline Susann was at first disturbed by the suggestion but after sleeping on it overnight, she decided to cut the pages from the manuscript. It is obviously hard to say whether *Once Is Not Enough* would still have been a bestseller if those pages had remained, but the fact is that it sold over 250,000 copies in hardcover alone and over 5,000,000 copies in paperback.

It is incidents like this that have enhanced Korda's reputation as not only a first-rate acquisitions editor (perhaps the best in the business) but also as a superb editor who can quickly move his pencil through a manuscript for the desired effect that he thinks will make the book work.

There is one other editor at Simon & Schuster who has an image within the industry that is strong and clear and that editor is Alice Mayhew who is vice president and associate publisher.

Alice Mayhew gained her fame as a result of editing *All the President's Men* and *The Final Days* by Bob Woodward and Carl Bernstein—two of the most successful books ever published.

Alice has a reputation for working hard. She is also perceived as an inspired editor who played a major role in the success of not only the Woodward/Bernstein books but William Shawcross's *Sideshow.*

Whereas Michael Korda is perceived as an editor who works quickly, Alice Mayhew has a reputation as an editor who works slowly.

I have worked with Alice Mayhew and one of the books I represented that she edited was *Breaking Cover* by Bill Gulley and Mary Ellen Reese. Alice did a superb job of editing the book and although it wasn't a major bestseller it was financially successful for Simon & Schuster and for the authors.

Although Alice Mayhew has a reputation for being an intellectual who is interested in books of a "heavy" nature, she has also proven herself with popular fiction and nonfiction. Obviously, because she edited *The Final Days* and *All the President's Men*, she is perceived as an editor who knows how to shape a bestseller.

Michael Korda and Alice Mayhew are the two most visible editors at Simon & Schuster. In an industry where the "star system" operates, they are perceived within the industry as two editorial stars.

Robert Gottlieb who holds the title of president and editor-in-chief of Alfred A. Knopf is perceived throughout the publishing industry as a man of superb judgment and excellent editorial skills who works carefully on his manuscripts and gets deeply involved in the books that he publishes.

I first met Bob Gottlieb in 1965 when he was a senior editor at Simon & Schuster which was shortly after the success of my first bestseller, *The Kennedy Wit.*

When Jay Sanford, my agent at the time, who headed the literary department at the Ashley Famous Agency (which subsequently became I.C.M.), told me that Bob Gottlieb and Peter Schwed, who was then the editor-in-chief at S & S, wanted to meet with me about a book, I was walking on air.

My meeting with Gottlieb and Schwed was cordial and warm and it was obvious that they wanted to do at least one book with the editor of the bestselling *The Kennedy Wit.* Out of that brief meeting emerged two book contracts—one for a book titled *The Johnson Humor* and one for a book titled *Dear 007.*

The Johnson Humor was to be for Lyndon Johnson what *The Kennedy Wit* had been for John F. Kennedy—a portrait of the president through his wit and humor. Unfortunately, the public did not think of Lyndon Johnson as a particularly witty man and the book was a crashing failure.

Dear 007, which was based on letters sent to the enormously successful motion picture character, Ian Fleming's James Bond, failed also.

I never did sell another book to Robert Gottlieb either at Simon & Schuster or after his arrival at Alfred Knopf. However, Peter Schwed and I have done much business together since that first encounter and I have represented many books for which he has been the editor. Peter Schwed is no longer the editor-in-chief at Simon & Schuster but despite the fact that he is near retirement, he still operates as effectively as he did before and he is one of the real gentlemen in the book publishing industry.

Bob Gottlieb's image within book publishing is probably enhanced by his manner of dress—which is always informal—and by his remarkable ability to develop many bestselling books which he personally edits. Gottlieb was the editor of Lauren Bacall's autobiography. In addition, he has edited such authors as Len Deighton, John Cheever, John Le Carré, Robert Stone and Doris Lessing.

I think it would be fair to say that Bob Gottlieb and Michael Korda are perceived within the industry as being two of the best acquisitions editors and certainly the most colorful editors working today. It is interesting to note that these two men worked together at Simon & Schuster.

Marc Jaffe, who for many years was the editor-in-chief at Bantam Books and is now executive vice president and editor-in-chief of Ballantine Books, is considered within publishing to be perhaps the smartest editor in the paperback business. When he was at Bantam, Marc Jaffe, along with the president of Bantam, Oscar Dystel, and other key executives who worked with them, was responsible for building that company into a major force in paperback publishing.

The list of bestsellers published by Bantam during the Oscar Dystel/Marc Jaffe years reads like a *Who's Who* of bestsellers. Among the books published by Bantam were *Valley of the Dolls, The Exorcist, Everything You Always Wanted to Know about Sex, Jaws, Sophie's Choice* and *The Complete Scarsdale Medical Diet.*

Jaffe is perceived within the publishing industry as a decent, hard working editor, a shrewd negotiator and a man who is intuitive about which books will sell and which books won't. To have had your book published by Marc Jaffe when he was editor-in-chief of Bantam was the ultimate. It was like reaching the top of Mt. Everest. What Michael Korda and Bob Gottlieb are to hardcover publishing, Marc Jaffe is to paperback publishing and like Korda and Gottlieb, Jaffe attracts the best agents and the best properties.

Jaffe has recently moved to Ballantine Books and although it is too early to assess his track record there, the early signs are that he has not lost his touch. *Gorky Park* was one of Jaffe's most recent acquisitions which quickly zoomed to the top of the bestseller list.

Don Fine is the president of Arbor House, a small but distinguished publishing firm. Fine has had a varied career in book publishing. He has worked for Scott Meredith, has been editor-in-chief at Dell Publishing Co. and was editor-in-chief at Coward, McCann & Geoghegan.

Arbor House was one of the few small, independent publishers functioning well, but a few years ago the Hearst Corporation purchased all of the Arbor House stock and Don Fine remained as president and publisher.

Don Fine is a short man in his mid-fifties who is well known within the publishing community and who is perceived on two levels. First, he has a reputation as one of the most brilliant fiction editors in the entire industry. The list of novelists who have been published by Arbor House under Fine's leadership is impressive. They include Ken Follett, Cynthia Freeman, Ernest Gann and Margaret Truman.

However, along with Don Fine's wonderful reputation as an editor and someone who knows intuitively how to promote and advertise fiction, he also has a reputation of being on occasion a difficult man to deal with. But in an imperfect world, Don Fine's moments of being difficult are certainly worth enduring in return for his solid judgment about books and book promotion. It would be only fair to say that many people in book publishing consider Don Fine to be one of the most accomplished practitioners of his trade.

I remember a luncheon conversation I had with Leona Nevler, who was then publisher of Fawcett Books, during which Don Fine's name came up. Leona made it quite clear to me that as far as she was concerned Fine was outstanding and that very few people were as good as he at discovering new talent and developing a bestseller out of that talent.

Don Fine's reputation in book publishing is not at all unlike the reputation Walter Minton had when he was president of the Putnam Publishing Group. Minton has since retired but when he was in control at G. P. Putnam's, he had a legendary reputation within the industry for being creative and at times difficult. More than one agent often commented about Walter Minton, "I know how to handle him." My own dealings with Walter Minton were surface ones, but as a result of the instances that I met with him, I can attest to his astuteness as a publisher.

Perhaps being difficult and brilliant go hand in hand but I don't think that is necessarily the case. A prime example of a man who is, in my judgment, brilliant but not difficult to work with is Larry Hughes, president and chief executive officer of William Morrow & Co.

Larry Hughes started his career as an editor at Pocket Books and then moved to William Morrow as editor-in-chief. Hughes is, I believe, perceived within the publishing industry as one of the true statesmen of the business and a man who runs a successful publishing firm that year after year turns out major bestsellers.

William Morrow was for many years an independent company but like virtually all the independent publishers of any size, they were subsequently bought by Scott, Foresman & Co., the large publisher of textbooks. The relationship between Scott, Foresman and William Morrow seemed a perfect match—a textbook publisher and a trade book publisher; but only recently Scott, Foresman sold William Morrow & Co. to the Hearst Corporation.

Morrow has published fiction and nonfiction successfully and also has three juvenile publishing divisions. Among the hardcover bestselling authors that Morrow has published over the years are Alvin Toffler, Sidney Sheldon, Ken Follett, Morris West, Joseph Wambaugh, Gail Sheehy, Ian Fleming, Mary Stewart, Christina Crawford, Shelley Winters, Doris Day, Jacqueline Susann, Dr. Herbert Benson and Nancy Friday.

I am a little biased toward Morrow and Larry Hughes because the truth is I have probably done more business as both agent and author with William Morrow than with any other publishing firm. The reasons for that are not complicated and most have to do with Larry Hughes.

Because he is an editor by training, Larry Hughes, even though he is president of a large publishing firm (William Morrow publishes approximately 280 trade hardcover books a year), he gets deeply involved in many of the manuscripts published by his company. Although I don't always agree with him, Larry Hughes senses intuitively what will and will not sell.

Hughes and Morrow are perceived within the publishing industry as being perhaps the most stable of all the publishing firms and in an industry where personnel (especially editors) have come and gone as if they were moving through a revolving door, Morrow has had editors who have remained on board for long periods of time; this, I believe, says something about the company and its president.

Hillel Black, the editor-in-chief at Morrow, has been with the firm for at least sixteen years; Jim Landis, who is the editorial director, has been there for fifteen years and Sherry Arden, associate publisher and vice president in charge of subsidiary rights, has been with Morrow for twelve years.

Larry Hughes is an even-tempered man who would have to be described as a reasonable person who listens to others and tries to make his decisions on the basis of all the facts. Hughes would be successful in virtually any industry for he has superb executive skills.

Larry Hughes, I think, works harder and longer than anybody in the business. His day usually ends at midnight having begun at around seven-thirty in the morning. Obviously, he is not in the office until midnight but rather at home in the evening reading manuscripts or out on a business engagement.

What is most important about the way Larry Hughes is perceived in the publishing industry relates to the success of William Morrow in making paperback and subsidiary sales. The book clubs and especially the paperback publishers respect the quality of the product that Morrow publishes and they know that Morrow as a firm and Larry Hughes as an individual are committed to making books work if it is at all possible.

I might add that on a personal level, Hughes has a delightful sense of humor. For that matter, so does Richard Snyder, president of Simon & Schuster. Actually, in order to survive and keep your head on your shoulders in book publishing, you have to have a sense of humor. The competition these days is so fierce that without it, you would not make it through the day, let alone weeks, months or years.

I don't know Robert L. Bernstein, president of Random House, very well because my own experience with Random House has been limited. Random House, of course, was for years associated with its dynamic president, the late Bennett Cerf, who was certainly the best- known publisher in the industry as a result of his many books and his television appearances on "What's My Line?" Cerf and his partner, Donald Klopfer, sold Random House to RCA and for many years it was a division of that large corporation. RCA has since sold Random House to Newhouse Newspapers.

Bob Bernstein has been the president of Random House for almost twenty years. Prior to joining Random House, Bernstein worked at Simon & Schuster in the sales department and later became sales manager of the Golden Records division. He joined Random House in 1958.

It is interesting to note that Simon & Schuster has been the breeding ground for many presidents of book publishing firms including Larry Hughes, the president of William Morrow; Seymour Turk, the chairman of Harry Abrams; Harold Roth who for many years was the president of

Grosset & Dunlap and Robert Gottlieb, the president of Alfred A. Knopf.

Bob Bernstein is perceived within the publishing industry as an excellent executive and an industry leader, an even-tempered man who does not impose his will on those who work for him but rather permits his editors and executives to function as independently as possible. Bernstein has often spoken out against the oppression of Russian writers and on issues involving freedom of the press.

Within the publishing industry, it is generally agreed that there is no love lost between Simon & Schuster and Random House, and I would assume that much of that is due to the fact that both Bob Bernstein and Bob Gottlieb once worked at Simon & Schuster. As a matter of fact, when Gottlieb left Simon & Schuster to go to Knopf, he took with him a goodly number of Simon & Schuster authors as well as some of their key personnel. This did not exactly cause Simon & Schuster to jump with joy.

Howard Kaminsky is the flamboyant president and publisher of Warner Books and is also the author with his wife of the bestselling novel, *The Glow,* written under the name of Brooks Stanwood. He is known for his delightful sense of humor and for being a hard working and friendly individual who has been instrumental in building Warner Books from nothing to a major force in the paperback industry.

Howard Kaminsky and Warner Books are perceived within the industry as being perhaps the most "Hollywood" of the book publishing firms with a flair for show business. This perception is due in part to the fact that Warner Books is a division of Warner Communications Co., which produces motion picture and television programs. On more than one occasion, I have had an author I represent say to me, "I would like to be published by Warner Books—they really know how to merchandise and promote a book."

The fact is that Warner's and Howard Kaminsky are excellent at promoting certain kinds of books and perhaps the best example of that recently was Richard Simmons's *Never-Say-Diet Book* which has sold more than 617,000 copies and has been on the major bestseller lists for over a year.

Kaminsky and Warner Books are perceived as publishers with a flair and in an industry where there aren't that many people with a flair, it obviously helps them in obtaining many book properties.

Lyle Stuart is the president of Lyle Stuart, Inc. which also includes Citadel Press. If I had to pick the one individual in publishing who was the most dramatic and controversial and is perceived to be exactly that way, it would have to be Lyle Stuart.

Lyle Stuart, Inc. is a small, independent publisher with a fantastic track record of bestselling books that have come out of nowhere—many of them created by Lyle Stuart himself. The company has published such bestsellers as Herb Cohen's *You Can Negotiate Anything, The Sensuous Woman,* and *The Sensuous Man.*

Lyle Stuart is a heavyset man with an outgoing and outspoken personality who loves to gamble and recently wrote a book that was published by his own firm giving his formula for success in gambling.

I have only been published once by Lyle Stuart. The book was *The Wit and Wisdom of Jimmy Carter* and it did not succeed which, of course, had nothing to do with Lyle Stuart or their ability to publish but rather because the public obviously didn't want to buy a book on the subject (probably because they didn't believe Jimmy Carter had much of either).

Lyle Stuart, Inc. bought Citadel Press a number of years ago. I have a soft spot in my heart for Citadel Press and its vice president for sales, Morris Sorkin, because it was Sorkin who agreed to publish *The Kennedy Wit* which was so instrumental in shaping my career.

Lyle Stuart runs a one-man show. He is aggressively involved in the advertising, jacket design and the editorial processes on most of the books published by his company. Most of the traditional agents do not do much business with Lyle Stuart for the simple reasons that he pays very small advances and also because, to say the least, he and his publishing firm have a controversial reputation.

Lyle Stuart is perceived within the industry as not the easiest man in the world to do business with and the number of authors who publish their *second* book with Stuart after publishing with him initially is very small. Among the many bestselling authors who have gone on to publish with other firms are Terry Garrity, author of *The Sensuous Woman,* Herb Cohen, author of *You Can Negotiate Anything* and Kitty Kelley, the author of *Jackie Oh!*

Peter Workman, the owner and president of Workman Publishing Co., is one of the classiest of the publishers. Since it was founded in 1967, Workman has built a remarkable firm that is totally independent of any conglomerate and the product that Peter Workman publishes every year reflects a highly intelligent organization with a remarkable ability to promote their merchandise.

Some of the successful books published by Workman Press over the years in addition to *The Official Preppy Handbook*, have included *"cat," Dieter's Guide to Weight Loss during Sex*, and *Sailing*.

Workman Publishing Company does not publish any fiction but rather concentrates in the areas in which they do best, which is why Peter Workman has been so successful as a publisher and has been able to maintain his independence. Although Workman Publishing is small compared to Simon & Schuster, Random House, Dell or William Morrow, it is perceived as a marvelous publishing operation which in many ways is the envy of the industry.

Workman himself is a bright, articulate individual and on the one occasion that I worked with him recently I found him to be sharp and to the point and very easy to work with.

Nat Wartels is the chairman of Crown Publishers and has to be described as the dean of book publishers because he has been at it for more than fifty years. Even today when Crown is such a large and successful publishing firm, Nat Wartels is still intimately involved in virtually every detail of the operation at an age when most of his contemporaries have long since retired. He continues to function as if he were a junior editor trying to work his way to the top. Nat Wartels is a bachelor and I don't think it would be unfair to say that he is married to his publishing company.

Nat Wartels and Crown are perceived as aggressive merchandisers who know how to get large numbers of books into the market place. Wartels is also regarded as being tight-fisted when it comes to spending money for advances to authors although of late he seems to be loosening the purse strings a little bit.

I can recall distinctly the first time I visited Nat Wartels's office at Crown which is located not in the high rent Madison Avenue district but rather on Park Avenue South which is considerably less expensive. Crown could easily afford the Madison Avenue rents but I would guess that it is against Nat Wartels's basic nature to spend unnecessary money on such things as rent or office surroundings.

What I remember most about my first visit to Nat's office was his desk. It was a mess. Papers and manuscripts were piled on top of papers and manuscripts and it really looked like a scene out of the Collier Brothers. I found it impossible to believe that this was the office of a man who owned one of the largest independent publishing firms, much less that Nat Wartels could find anything on his desk. But obviously he has been able to function that way successfully for many years.

I like Nat Wartels and I think most people in the publishing industry feel the same way. Nat Wartels and the president of Crown, Alan Mirken, have been trailblazers in so many areas in book publishing that it would take a separate book just to discuss them.

However, one of their more remarkable successes has been the development of their Outlet Book Company for remainder books. It was Nat Wartels and Alan Mirken who pioneered the development of remainder books whereby publishers have the opportunity to sell their overstock books at a low cost and the book buying public has the opportunity to buy those books at a fraction of their original price.

It is altogether possible that by the time this book is published, Nat Wartels will have finally retired, but I believe that within the publishing community, Wartels is perceived to be a man who will never retire—which will be good for book publishing.

I have obviously left out many of the characters who are active in the publishing community today because of limited space and also because I felt that the ones discussed typify the most interesting personalities in book publishing today, and I think they are perceived that way by their contemporaries.

I offer no apologies or qualifications for the descriptions I have written or the comments I have made except to say that these are very subjective judgments. This chapter must be considered a personal observation by one writer and agent and certainly not gospel.

The Literary Agents

MANHATTAN is loaded with literary agents. In the current issue of the *LMP* there are more than 270 agents listed and there are many agents whose names do not appear—including one of the more successful, Morton Janklow, and my own firm.

The reason Bill Adler Books is not listed is that we would prefer not to receive unsolicited manuscripts and letters from would-be writers and authors.

One of the reasons always given for the necessity of having a literary agent is that writers are not business people—they are artists, creative individuals—and therefore they cannot be concerned with or be expected to understand the intricacies of negotiation or business dealings with publishers. That is nonsense! Many of the writers and authors I have represented are superb business people and could easily act on their own behalf. However, they chose not to and, like most of the writers in this country, they have preferred to leave their business dealings in the hands of others—the literary agents.

Even the name literary agent is a misnomer. Many of the agents are not literary at all but rather plain and simple salesmen, no different from someone selling insurance. Their job is to find a publisher, negotiate a contract and see the book through to its final publication.

There are literary agents in other cities besides Manhattan. They are located in Washington, D.C., Atlanta, Chicago and Los Angeles, to mention but a few cities where there has been a remarkable growth in the number of literary agents over the past five years.

It is with some trepidation that I venture into that "no man's land" in giving an opinion on who are the best literary agents. I would be less than honest if I did not say that obviously I do not know them all but over the course of the years, I have worked with many, met many and heard of the rest.

I would have to say that I think the top five literary agencies are Scott Meredith, Morton Janklow, International Creative Management (ICM), Sterling Lord and Writers House.

Scott Meredith may be the best literary agent in history. He has represented such heavyweights as Norman Mailer, Ellery Queen, Carl Sagan, Morris West, Ernest Gann, Taylor Caldwell, Gerald Greene, Arthur C. Clarke, Abby Mann, and Garry Wills.

Meredith has the largest of the literary agencies and probably represents more books each year than any other literary agent. One of the best negotiators I have seen in action (and I can speak from experience because he has on a number of occasions represented me as a writer), was Scott Meredith who developed the idea of auctioning books. The auctioning concept was radical for book publishing when it was first introduced, but it was a brilliant idea and it has now become standard industry practice.

In an auction situation an agent will submit simultaneously to a number of publishers the same book proposal, outline or manuscript. Each of the publishers receiving the proposal will be asked to submit its offer for the book by a prearranged date and time. The publisher that puts in the highest bid for the book gets the honor (and hopefully the profits) of publishing the book.

Before the auction concept was developed by Scott Meredith, most agents dealt with one publisher at a time on a particular book—but the auctioning changed all of that. In the beginning publishers were up in arms (to put it mildly) about book auctions, but that has changed and publishers have now learned to live with the auction just as the tennis player assumes that "tennis elbow" will eventually come with the game.

Another Scott Meredith "first" is their manuscript evaluation department. For a fee the Scott Meredith Agency will read an unsolicited manuscript from any writer and evaluate its potential.

Meredith's is not the only agency that will evaluate manuscripts for the would-be writer but he certainly created the concept and it has become a big factor in his successful business. Evaluating manuscripts for a fee is, of course, controversial. Many people in book publishing object to charging writers for a judgment on their work, but I happen to think it is a good idea. There are thousands of writers around the country starving for some professional assessment of their literary ability, and this is one way they can have someone give them advice on their work besides their mother, grandmother or favorite aunt.

A really good agent has to know which book publisher is best for which kind of book and which editor is looking for a particular type of book. Scott Meredith has always had a finely tuned sense of the best places for various kinds of book properties and his sales records on behalf of his clients are remarkably high.

Certainly one of the most successful literary agents is Morton Janklow. Janklow was an attorney who sort of drifted into book publishing as a result of being an attorney for the *New York Times* columnist William Safire. Safire asked Janklow to represent one of his book deals a number of years ago and that was the beginning of what has become perhaps the hottest literary agent around today.

Morton Janklow's list of clients reads like a *Who's Who* of book publishing. Among his authors are Judith Krantz, Sidney Sheldon, Linda Goodman, Barbara Taylor Bradford and Tad Szulc.

Janklow, because of his strong ties to Hollywood and show business people (his wife, Linda, is the daughter of the legendary Hollywood director, Mervyn LeRoy), has many celebrity and show business clients. Among the show business personalities that Janklow has represented in the literary field are Henry Fonda and Susan Strasberg.

Janklow is a hardhitting negotiator who strikes a tough deal on behalf of his clients. Because he is also an attorney, Janklow understands the art of negotiation better than most literary agents. He has become a celebrity in his own right and has been profiled in the *New Yorker* magazine, and his name frequently appears in the newspapers.

It is not easy to get Morton Janklow as your agent and it is fair to say that at this stage of the game, he can be very selective about whom he will represent.

Morton Janklow recently negotiated one of the largest deals in publishing history in which Barbara Taylor Bradford received an advance of

$3,000,000 for a two-book contract with Doubleday. Barbara Taylor Bradford's first novel, *A Woman of Substance,* sold some 45,000 copies in hardcover and about three million in paperback. The advance from Doubleday for her first novel was $25,000 but paperback rights were bought by Avon for $315,000.

ICM is one of the largest talent agencies in the country, equal in size to the William Morris Agency. ICM has a literary department that is enormously successful. The agents who work in the ICM literary department include such well-known agents as Lynn Nesbit, Roberta Pryor and Esther Newberg, among others. These are powerful and important women in the publishing industry. Among the authors and personalities that ICM has represented in the literary field are John Cheever, Tom Wolfe, Arthur Miller, Henry Kissinger, Tennessee Williams, Shelley Winters, Candice Bergen, Shirley MacLaine, Robert and Peter Benchley, John Barth and Donald Barthelme.

The William Morris literary department, headed by Owen Laster, is also a superb agency but I think that the ICM organization has proven to be stronger in the literary market place over the last few years.

Sterling Lord, a former magazine editor, has been a major literary agent in New York for many years. His reputation is impeccable, and he and his associates have represented many of the biggest names published in the country including Richard Goodwin, F. Lee Bailey, Ben Bradlee, Barbara Howar, Jane Howard, Dick Schaap, Doris Kearns, Jimmy Breslin, David McCullough, Pete Axthelm, Howard Fast, Dick Francis, Erica Jong, Arthur Koestler and Pierre Salinger.

I have always thought that Sterling Lord had a distinct advantage over every other agent because of his name. Who wouldn't want to be represented by a man named Sterling Lord? That is impressive to begin with.

Several years ago, I was asked to meet with the former Watergate jurist Judge John Sirica who at the time was thinking about writing a book. Judge Sirica interviewed two agents—myself and Sterling Lord. Sterling Lord became Judge Sirica's agent and, although I would like to have represented the man who is credited with causing the downfall of Richard Nixon, I always felt that Judge Sirica was well served in selecting Mr. Lord. The book, *To Set the Record Straight,* was published by W.

W. Norton and became a national bestseller—bringing heavy profits for the publisher, Judge Sirica and, of course, the agent, Sterling Lord.

An amusing sidelight to my meeting with Judge Sirica was his nervousness about even discussing the possibility of writing a book about his Watergate experiences for fear that it might sound as if he were trying to "cash in" as so many others had done before him—John Dean, H. R. Haldeman and Nixon himself. Because Judge Sirica did not want it leaked to the press that he was contemplating writing a book, I had to take a suite at the Hay Adams Hotel in Washington so that the judge and I could meet over a quiet lunch in complete secrecy.

My impression of Judge Sirica was that he was a tough judge and I recall commenting to my wife, Gloria, when I returned to New York after my meeting with him that I wouldn't want to appear before him in court even if it were only a traffic ticket.

Not only did Sterling Lord wind up with the famed jurist as a client but I was out of pocket for air fare to and from Washington and that suite at the Hay Adams Hotel.

Writers House is headed by an articulate man by the name of Al Zuckerman whose clients include bestselling novelists Ken Follett and Anne Tolstoi Wallach.

When you represent an author like Ken Follett or Judith Krantz (whose agent is Morton Janklow) or Norman Mailer (whose agent is Scott Meredith), you are representing a major profit center for your agency. Follett, Krantz and Mailer are prolific writers and their agents are guaranteed commissions worldwide every year.

Publishers have enormous respect for Al Zuckerman. They believe (with justification) that he cares about the books and authors he represents and that in many ways he is almost an adjunct to their editorial processes.

Not every agent gets involved in the editorial process—many make the sale and are never heard from again. But in the case of the five I have just mentioned, they do in many instances become involved.

A good agent will spend time with the author and the publisher on the title of the book and the structure of the book, and a truly concerned literary agent with some talent of his own will actually get involved in the writing of the manuscript with suggestions to the author and recommendations that will make the manuscript better and stronger.

Obviously, the selection of the five best literary agents is purely subjective on my part and there is no doubt that many people in the industry will disagree with me. But I think they are the five best and any author who is represented by any of them is in good hands.

There are other excellent literary agents and they deserve to be mentioned. They include Henry Morrison and Richard Curtis (both of whom used to work for Scott Meredith), Jay Acton, Philip Spitzer, Robert Lantz, Knox Burger and Candida Donadio.

The first and most important thing to understand about agents is that they are essentially commissioned salespeople. If they don't make the sale they don't get their commission. There aren't any legitimate agents that I know of who charge a fee for representing your book. Although the Scott Meredith Agency does charge a fee for reading and evaluating unpublished manuscripts, that is a separate department at the Meredith Agency.

Most agents still charge a commission of 10%. That's 10% of every dollar received by the author (advances and royalties) as well as 10% of all other income earned by the author from the book, including television and motion picture rights. In other words, if the author makes a total of $100,000 then the agent who charges 10% earns $10,000. The agent has a clause written into the contract with the publisher spelling out the author/agent relationship in connection with the book under contract (See Appendix).

Most agents (but certainly not all) belong to an association called the Society of Authors Representatives Inc. (SAR) which loosely monitors the activities of its member agents.

More and more agents are beginning to charge 15% (we were one of the first) simply because the cost of doing business for an agent has gone up like everything else and it seemed ridiculous for agents to charge the same commission in the eighties that they were charging in the fifties. Among the agents now charging most of their clients 15% are Knox Burger, Jay Acton, James Seligmann and Sanford J. Greenburger.

Some agents require contracts with their authors for one, two or three years. A typical agent/author contract is to be found in the Appendix. Among the agencies that ask their authors to sign contracts are Scott Meredith, Sterling Lord, ICM and William Morris.

Bill Adler Books does not require a contract with an author which may not be the best business judgment in the world but we prefer it that way. If the author doesn't want to do any more business with us (or if we don't want to do any more business with the author) then we would rather sever the relationship. Life is too short to try to make bad relationships work.

Should you sign a contract with an agent?

With some agents you have no choice. If you want them to represent you, then you will have to sign their contract. Like anything else there are good agents (even great agents), agents who are so-so and agents who can do you more harm than good.

When I was the editorial director for *Playboy*'s book division, I had the opportunity to assess agents from the other side of the desk and I was often surprised by the lack of judgment of some agents. Agents would submit books to us at Playboy Press that were obviously not the kind of books we published at a male-oriented book publishing operation. What were we going to do at Playboy with a book on needlepoint or gourmet cooking for the single woman?

The first sign of a good agent is that he or she knows the market and knows which books to submit to which publishers. Even if you had the greatest novel since *Sons and Lovers* it wouldn't make much sense to submit that book to Frederick Fell or Bobbs-Merrill or Workman Publishing since they publish virtually no fiction and have had little or no success with novels.

A smart agent and an agent who is well tuned in will know which editors and publishers are looking for what books. An agent who knows what is going on isn't going to try to sell a book on physical fitness to Farrar, Straus or Scribner's when those two fine old publishing firms have virtually no success with that sort of book.

First an agent must know the publishers and the editors—what they like to publish and what they publish well, and secondly an agent must be a good and convincing salesman who believes in his property and its potential. Any agent who describes *every* book that he represents as "the greatest" will quickly destroy his credibility. Every book is not a bestseller and although I represent 120 books a year I try to use superlatives sparingly so that when I say a book is the best it will have more meaning.

Needless to say I have been wrong on occasion. I have touted books as bestsellers and they weren't. When I sold Dr. Herbert Benson's second book, *The Mind/Body Effect,* following his number one bestseller, *The*

Relaxation Response, to Simon & Schuster for a very healthy six-figure advance, I said it would be a bestseller. Although the book did all right, it wasn't a bestseller.

On the other hand, I never thought that my own *Letters from Camp* would be the bestseller it was, and I was as surprised as the publisher.

It is difficult to define salesmanship, although there have certainly been enough books written on the subject.

Jeffrey Feinman, a successful sales promotion executive and prolific author, recently published a book with Doubleday titled *The Money Lists*. In the book, Feinman lists the ten best salesmen and he was kind enough to include me on that list (number five). I'm not so sure that I am one of the ten best, but as an agent I have developed certain sales techniques which work for me—as I know they do for other agents who are excellent salespeople.

Here are the rules of successful selling in book publishing. If your agent doesn't employ them, it is time to think about getting another agent.

1. Look the buyer straight in the eye. Shifty eyes hardly ever make a sale.
2. Know what you are selling. You can't sell a book about underwater swimming if you haven't read the book proposal. (You would be surprised at the number of agents who never read the outlines for the books they are selling.)
3. Don't talk too much and know when it is time to shut up.
4. Don't oversell. Agents who continually use such words as "fantastic," "great," "super," and "marvelous" aren't selling anybody.
5. When you have made the sale, change the subject. Talk about something else. On more than one occasion, I have seen editors change their minds because the agent continued to talk about the book and gave the editor pause for second thoughts.
6. Without using too many words point out the reasons you think the book will sell. Base your reasoning on logic and an understanding of the market rather than emotions.
7. Don't appear nervous or seem anxious. Cool cats really are more effective salespeople.

Agents have to be good negotiators because in many cases their ability to negotiate can mean hundreds of thousands (even millions) of dollars for their author. It's as easy to negotiate a $100,000 deal as it is a $10,000 contract, and the best agents are the ones who are at ease with any dollar figure.

The main factor in negotiating an advance for a book is your judgment on how anxious the buyer is for the book. Like the classic question, "Which came first, the chicken or the egg?" the key judgment call every agent has to make in negotiating the price of a book is who should quote the first price—the buyer or the seller.

Often the editor will ask the agent, "How much do you want for that book?" The agent must then determine whether he should quote a price for the book or let the editor do it. If the agent should say $50,000 and the editor was prepared to pay $75,000 then the agent just lost $25,000 for his client.

Most good agents play it by ear when negotiating the advance for a book, but as a general rule I think the most effective negotiators among the agents will let the publisher make the first move.

The agent who is a good negotiator knows when to close the deal and finalize the sale. When an editor has been authorized to buy a book from an agent, the conversation between editor and executive goes something like this:

Editor: I think we should buy Bill Adler's new book.

Publisher: I agree with you. How much do you think we can get it for?

Editor: Maybe $50,000.

Publisher: Offer him $40,000.

Editor: $40,000?

Publisher: Try to get it for $40,000 but you can go as high as $50,000 if you have to.

It is obviously a plus for the editor in the eyes of his boss if he can secure Bill Adler's next book for $40,000 or $42,500 or $45,000.

All the aware agents know that when a publisher makes an offer it is usually not the final offer. Even when an editor says, "that's my final offer" he or she doesn't necessarily mean it. Money negotiating in book publishing is a cat and mouse game.

If you are an author, you should be aware that your book is not considered as accepted by the publisher until the final advance payment has been made. Unless your contract has a specific clause stating that the advance doesn't have to be returned or can be returned from the first proceeds of a sale to another publisher, you must return the advance payments you have already received if the manuscript is not accepted.

Unless you are a good client or an important author, the agent may not return his percentage of the advance to the publisher—and that is especially true when it comes to an author who does not write the book at all. All this means is that an author can write a book and have it rejected by the publisher and unless his agent finds another publisher, he will be out the agent's commission. From the agent's point of view, he sold the book and is therefore entitled to his commission for making the sale.

One of the distinct advantages of being represented by a superagent is that the publishers have a tendency to be a little gentler and more understanding, not necessarily because of the author but because they don't want to ruffle the feathers of a superagent who they will need many times in the future for those big properties.

Most agents are honest and although they handle millions of dollars of their clients' money, I can't recall any scandal involving a literary agent.

Monies (advances and royalties) that are due to the author are paid to the author's agent who deducts his commission and then pays the author. This is the way it has always been done in book publishing and the reason is, I guess, that it is easier for an author to get his money from an agent than vice versa. It's not that most authors aren't honest but there is always the distinct possibility that the author would spend the agent's commission before he had the chance to pay him.

If you are going to be represented by an agent whom you have never heard of before, don't be shy about asking the agent who he represents or even checking with someone in the publishing industry. Agents are not licensed and it's a good idea not to have anyone represent you before you know something about that agent.

Many agents are former editors as are John Cushman, Robert Lescher, Ned Leavitt, Clyde Taylor, Jonathan Dolger, Sterling Lord and Diane Cleaver. As a result of their editorial background and expertise, they can be of considerable assistance in the process of writing your book.

Most agents use foreign agents in England, Japan, Germany and the rest of Europe. The foreign agents charge 10%, which is deducted from the author's share of foreign sales. That means most authors are paying a commission of 20% (if their American agent charges 10%) and 25% (if their American agent charges 15%) for books sold abroad.

Movie and television sales are handled one of three ways:

1. The agent sells the property directly to the motion picture or television producer.
2. The agent uses a California-based agent (See Appendix) who is closer to the motion picture and television scene and who knows better who is looking for what, and splits his commission with the California agent.
3. The agent uses a California agent and the author is charged the California agent's 10% commission as well as his literary agent's commission.

Some agents take a long time (or at least it seems like a long time to the authors) to respond to a manuscript or a book proposal. It is not uncommon to hear an author complain that he sent his outline to Agent X and it's been four weeks and he still hasn't heard from the agent as to whether he likes the proposal and will take it on. Don't sign up with an agent who takes too long to make a decision about your work. Any agent, no matter how busy he or she is, should be able to make a decision relating to a manuscript within two weeks.

Another frequent complaint from writers is that they can never get their agent on the phone, especially if their agent happens to be one of the superagents and the author is not a "heavy hitter." Frankly, that is just plain rude (and not very good business manners) so if that kind of tactic annoys you, go with a less powerful agent who will return your calls.

Finally, the good agent is the agent who is persistent and doesn't give up.

Agents are like all of us and they can get discouraged easily. Not all publishing sales are made on the first or second or even third submission. If you believe in the book property, you have to keep at it. I have made many sales after the twentieth and even the fortieth submission.

There are still many books that are sold without an agent. Some people use their attorneys just to negotiate their contract, while other authors handle everything themselves. On balance, it is best to use an agent, and most publishers would rather negotiate with an agent who they believe will handle the contract more professionally than an author acting without an agent.

The old adage that a lawyer who acts on his own behalf has a fool for a client is pretty close to the truth when it comes to an author representing himself.

Many editors who write books use agents; for example:

Michael Korda (Simon & Schuster)—Lynn Nesbit at ICM

Howard Kaminsky (Warner Books)—John Hawkins at the Paul Reynolds Agency

Herbert Katz (M. Evans)—Henry Morrison Agency

An editor certainly knows enough about the business to be able to represent himself but the wise editor who is also an author makes the right decision when he has an agent acting on his behalf.

We are all too subjective and involved to be cold, logical and rational about the books we write. It is better to have somebody else speak for us.

The Trouble with Being an Agent

IF I had to do it all over again, I am not really sure that I would become a literary agent. The problem with being a literary agent is not complicated. It is the authors.

Now don't misunderstand me. I have great respect and admiration for writers who pursue their craft with determination and talent but the truth is that most people who earn their livings as writers are a little nuts—perhaps not certifiable—but certainly not exactly your average American.

First of all, most writers are convinced that everyone is against them—the publisher, the editor, the reviewer and certainly their agent.

For most writers it is torture to sit alone for six or eight hours a day in front of a typewriter. I have yet to meet the writer who really enjoys the process of writing. They may enjoy the finished product or the creative experience or the ego gratification that comes from having their words read and considered by others but the actual physical process of writing—the lonely hours in front of a piece of paper are terrible at best. That is why the alcoholic consumption rate among writers is way above the average, why the divorce rate among writers is also way above the national average, why perhaps more writers spend time with their shrinks than any other segment of the population.

The other thing about writers, or authors as they like to be referred to, is that they are usually broke. Half of our time at Bill Adler Books is spent trying to unravel the financial complications of our authors. In the course of any given week, we are certain to receive phone calls, telegrams or letters that plaintively state:

> "My taxes are due on the 15th and I am desperate for $8,000."
>
> "I don't think I can meet next month's mortgage payment."
>
> "My daughter's tuition bill has come due and if I don't get $5,000 by Tuesday, I'll have to put her back in public school."

It's not that many authors don't earn a lot of money; they do. But for some reason that continues to astound me, their cash flow is always horrendous. Perhaps that's due in part to the fact that they get large amounts of money in lump sums and maybe they figure that if they receive $40,000 in November, they are going to receive another $40,000 in January, February, etc.

Obviously, it doesn't work that way.

Most publishers pay royalties twice a year and it can be a long time between royalty payments, especially if you haven't made arrangements to put your money away for those days when royalty payments are not coming in.

The other problem with the writer is ego. You have to have an enormous ego to want to make your living as a writer. Your ego has to tell you, "Hey, what I have to say is plenty interesting or even sensational and I would like other people to read my words." Writers in this respect are not any different from actors or anyone else who makes a living performing for the public. The truth is that writers are performers, only in their case they are performing with words, not with action or music.

A friend of mine once asked me to describe what it was like to represent authors, and I told him this hypothetical story that probably best describes what it is like to be a literary agent.

If I were having lunch with an author I represented and turned to him and said, "Bob, I didn't want to tell you this before but I am afraid now is the time to break the news. I have terminal cancer."

Bob, my author/client, would undoubtedly immediately respond with, "Thanks for telling me but how will that affect my book?"

This hypothetical story is the best summation of the relationship between writers and the rest of the world. Everything revolves around their book.

If they go to Des Moines to visit their mother and their latest book isn't in the bookstores, it is a conspiracy against them. If the *New York Times* doesn't review their book, it is because they are Irish and the *New York Times* doesn't like Irish writers. If Phil Donahue won't have them on his program, it's because Donahue is really shallow and doesn't understand the hidden meaning of their book. And, if the ultimate insult of all occurs, if their book doesn't sell or, to put it more bluntly, is a bomb, it is obviously because the publisher didn't do his job, the reviewer didn't understand the book and most of all, the reading public has the intelligence of a six-year-old.

Another thing about writers is that they are the world's worst procrastinators. Perhaps this has to do with the fact that most writers really don't like the process of writing and that they can find any excuse known to man not to have to sit and begin to write. Again, that is probably because it is such a lonely, difficult job to sit at a typewriter.

Most publishers give six months, a year, two years or even longer for an author to write his book, and it has been my experience that most writers never begin writing when they should and are often late with their manuscripts because they took so long in getting started.

But with all that I have said about writers, I think they are still the most interesting and fascinating people to deal with and to know. They are bright, creative individuals who are far above the norm and who, although they are often neurotic and plagued by more phobias than you can list, are still delightful people to be with.

If you are thinking of a full-time career as a writer, you must be prepared for rejection, rejection, rejection and more rejection. That is probably the greatest cross writers have to bear. Even the literary greats face rejection and have books that fail, plays that don't make it to Broadway or movies that should never have been released. The only weapons writers have are their words and their ability to express themselves. That doesn't always work nor does it always get the acceptance from the public that the writer had hoped for.

Within the last five years, however, a wonderful thing has happened to authors. Many of them have become celebrities and that, of course, is because of television.

Perhaps the first author to become a television celebrity was Jacqueline Susann, the talented writer who has probably sold more books in a shorter space of time than any other novelist. Jacqueline Susann's best-selling books were *Every Night Josephine*, *Valley of the Dolls*, *Once Is Not Enough*, *Dolores*, and *The Love Machine*.

There is no question that Jacqueline Susann's numerous appearances, starting when *Valley of the Dolls* was first published fifteen years ago, with Johnny Carson and Merv Griffin and other such television personalities were instrumental in making Jacqueline Susann not only one of the most successful novelists of our time but also a major media personality. She was recognized in supermarkets, in department stores, on airplanes. She wasn't just a novelist, she was a star.

Television has made media stars out of a long list of writers whose faces are as familiar as their names and their books. They include such people as Truman Capote, Judith Krantz, Norman Mailer, Nancy Friday, Dr. Wayne Dyer, Herb Cohen and Milton Friedman.

Before the advent of television, a writer's name appeared in print and occasionally a well-known author would appear at a local bookstore to sign some books or to lecture before a Kiwanis club but never in the history of the printed word have writers had the opportunity to become media celebrities and, with some exceptions, most authors love it.

Many times I have authors in my office who, even before they tell me what they have written, make comments to the effect that they are great on television or that they really know how to handle themselves on talk shows or that they have a warm, outgoing personality that comes over great. This is all before I even have a chance to look at their material to find out if they have the most important requirement to be an author—the ability to write.

In a way all of this is sad as well as good. It is sad that we put such emphasis on the ability of writers to be able to promote what they have written, but it is good because television has helped the book industry open the doors to more people instead of just to those who read the *New York Times, Saturday Review* or *The Atlantic.* Awareness is the key and it is impossible to interest anybody in anything if he is not aware of what you are about. Certainly, television has helped enormously in changing all of that.

The tragedy is the talented writer who has something really important to say but has a terrible stutter or some other speech impediment or some physical problem that limits his or her ability to promote the book on television.

Not every book should be or is promoted on television but if Dr. Wayne Dyer had not been such a dynamic personality, he would not have become a millionaire overnight as a result of not only what he wrote but his remarkable ability to promote—especially on television.

It was only a few years ago that Wayne Dyer was just another clinical psychologist. Then he teamed up with the delightful and aggressive literary agent Arthur Pine and the rest became publishing history. Since the publication of his first book, *Your Erroneous Zones,* in 1976, Dr. Dyer's titles have included *Pulling Your Own Strings* and *The Sky's the Limit,* and his books sold more than one million copies.

Wayne Dyer had something to say but I am sure he would be the first to admit that, as an author, his career was made by television.

Some day, I am sure, if they are not already doing it, the Columbia School of Journalism or some other outstanding journalism school will offer a course on promoting your novel on television or how to get media attention for your definitive history of how Napoleon met his Waterloo.

I do believe that a new respect has developed in this country for people who write, whether they are crusading journalists like Woodward and Bernstein, or masters of language and political commentary like William Safire, or prolific playwrights like Neil Simon or brilliant novelists like John Irving.

Those who make their living from the published word or the dramatized word are no longer thought of as people who cannot earn a living. It was only a short time ago that a father would be sent into the depths of despair if his daughter told him she was going to marry an actor or a writer because it was assumed that he would never earn a living and that you would be saddled with their financial well-being for the rest of your life.

That has changed dramatically and although most writers in this country still have to struggle, the list of writers who have become wealthy overnight or in a short space of time has grown tremendously.

7

The Trouble with Lawyers

IF I had to describe my mission professionally and personally, I would have to say it is to get books published. Essentially that is the business I am in. Nothing gives me more gratification than to have a book published—even if it is not successful—that I was involved with, either as an agent or as a writer or as a packager.

I remember distinctly the fantastic pleasure I experienced when my first hardcover book, *Letters from Camp,* was published way back in the fifties. Although I must admit it was a joy that was almost muted by an episode that took place at Doubleday's Bookstore on Fifth Avenue and Fifty-Third Street.

The very day that *Letters from Camp* was published, I decided to go to that famous Doubleday store at nine in the morning to see how many copies of my book they had in stock. I quietly counted the number of copies and it came to twelve. I made a mental note of the number and decided to come back at five that day after I left work at the advertising agency where I was employed as an account executive.

Promptly at five, I returned to Doubleday's and began to count the number of copies of *Letters from Camp* they now had in stock. To my dismay, I discovered they had fifteen copies.

During the day, three people had returned copies and if that weren't enough to end my career in book publishing, nothing else would have done it.

Fortunately, I persevered and although my first experience at Doubleday was minus three copies, *Letters from Camp* went on to sell more than one million copies in its paperback edition.

I love books and book people and I have always felt that the final determining factor in the success or failure of a book should be the book buying public, which leads me to lawyers.

I can't speak about all lawyers because I'm certainly not that familiar with lawyers who specialize in real estate, international, criminal or corporate law, but I do believe that I can discuss with some accuracy the attorneys who are involved in book publishing. I am specifically referring to the lawyers who are called on by writers or celebrities to either represent them or to look over their contracts for any problems despite the fact that the author or celebrity had been represented by a literary agent.

I have no quarrel with anyone who desires to have an attorney look something over for him before he signs it, but I do object violently to lawyers who advise their clients about book contracts when in reality they know absolutely nothing about book contracts and even less about book publishing.

When a literary agent represents an author, he or she usually makes those changes in a contract that are in the best interests of the author. Most literary agents understand all the clauses involved in even the most complicated contracts and are able to interpret and understand all of the words printed on the contract pages. Yet, despite the fact that a literary agent has negotiated hundreds of contracts, authors still persist in calling in attorneys to read the contract and get into the act.

Without exaggerating, I would estimate that I have negotiated more than 2,000 contracts over the span of my publishing career and I doubt if there is any attorney walking the streets of Manhattan, or any other city for that matter, who has handled even 10% of that number.

A few months ago, I sold a book for a minor celebrity for a small advance of only $5,000. The celebrity was happy with the advance and the basic terms of the contract but he then turned the contract over to his attorney as he put it for "a quick look." That "quick look" turned into months of arduous negotiation and renegotiation between the attorney for the client and the attorneys for the publishing firm. I would venture to say that the celebrity's bill from his attorney for that contract is easily $1,500 and the deal has still not been finalized.

There are not that many attorneys, at least in Manhattan, who really understand book publishing. Some of those who do are Ron Konecky, Harold Schiff, Eugene Winick, Seymour Reitknecht, Egon Dumler, Paul Sawyer, Paul Sherman, John Diamond and Charles Rembar.

It is especially ludicrous to have a book contract gone over by a general attorney who doesn't understand most of the lingo used in book publishing, has no knowledge at all about the distribution system or the discount structure and probably doesn't even know what a book club is. I have had attorneys who have represented well-known people ask me questions that indicated a total lack of knowledge of book publishing. And yet these attorneys rarely tell their clients the truth—that publishing is not their province and that they can contribute little or nothing. Rather, these attorneys are willing to take their time, the client's time, the agent's time and the publisher's time discussing points that cannot be changed.

I have recently made it a policy that after I have negotiated a contract I step aside from the situation when the client brings in an attorney. If the client wants to waste time and money with a lawyer then that lawyer can deal directly with the publisher and the publisher's attorney. I have done my job and I am not going to waste any more time with attorneys who are really only in the act to create fees.

If I sound like an angry middle-aged man on this subject, I am. The trouble with lawyers is they hardly ever say to a client in all honesty, "You don't need me" or "Why don't you find someone who is a specialist in this kind of law" or perhaps the most simple of all, "Your agent obviously knows more about book publishing than I do."

This is not to say that when there is a problem in connection with a book—a lawsuit or some kind of litigation stemming from a contract or the publication of the book—that you should not employ a lawyer. Obviously, you should.

If you are a writer and you are being sued for libel or plagiarism or you are being sued by the book publisher for violating your contract, then by all means get an attorney.

Although we have never sued anybody, we have been sued and on those occasions we certainly used attorneys to handle our cases.

Too many authors get nervous and frightened when they are confronted with a ten-, twelve- or fourteen-page contract from a book publisher. Panic sets in and that is when they are driven to get an attorney. It isn't necessary in most cases. I have seen more than one publishing deal die aborning because the attorney was making too many waves and raising too many unnecessary questions to the point where the publisher decided it wasn't worth it.

Some of the larger literary agencies like William Morris and ICM employ their own attorneys within the firm and these attorneys are well equipped to make judgments on publishing contracts. I should say in all fairness, however, that many of the contracts are much too long and much too complicated. Some of them read like life insurance policies or an apartment lease.

Some of the publishers have cut their contracts down to two to four pages so that they are easy to follow and understand. Among the shorter and easier to read contracts are those from Bobbs-Merrill, Grosset & Dunlap, Caroline House, McGraw-Hill and Thomas Nelson.

Some of the longer contracts and ones with clauses that seem to me to be unnecessary and in some instances confusing are from Simon & Schuster; Little, Brown; Farrar, Straus; Coward, McCann; Doubleday and Putnam's.

There is no reason for any book publishing contract to be longer than four pages; and with a little discipline and tightening up, that could easily be accomplished with every publishing firm, especially in an industry that is all about writing. The ability to write a simple contract should not be that big a problem.

I know most people won't believe this but I can recall representing a book where the legal negotiations on matters concerning the contract took twice as long as the actual writing of the book, and in that instance, as in most of the instances involving attorneys and book contracts, the changes finally wrought by the attorneys didn't put one extra dollar into the pocket of the author. As a matter of fact, because of legal fees it took a few dollars *out* of the author's pocket.

I don't care what anybody else in the publishing industry may say, there are only three elements that are essential to the success of the book. Two are written into the contract and the other is in the hands of the gods.

The two elements that are in the contract are the advance and the royalties. Those are the payout clauses. The advance gives you the money to make the book worth doing and the royalties give you the opportunity to make real money after the book succeeds. I include in the royalty clauses subsidiary income from book clubs, paperback sales, foreign rights and other areas. If you have a good advance, a good royalty scale and an equitable share of the subsidiary income, then that is all you should really be concerned about. And if you have a good agent, you don't need an attorney to be involved.

What, of course, is in the hands of the gods and what no attorney or anyone else can do very much about is the way you write the book, the competition at the time your book is published and, most important of all, the publisher's enthusiasm for the book and the publisher's desire to get behind the book when it is on the market.

Many books are dead before they are published. As a matter of fact, many books are dead the day the contract is signed. By "dead" I mean the publisher is not going to do very much with the book and although he will publish it, he really has no intention of making much of the property.

Obviously, the publisher will not tell you that when you sign the contract. Like the Hollywood agent, the publisher will smile and assure you he is going to make you and your book a star. But in most cases, that is just not true. A healthy percentage of the books that publishers sign up, they know are going to go nowhere; and they hope that maybe the book will break even.

Needless to say, they never tell this to the author and most authors labor under the illusion that the publisher is going to do everything he can to make the book a success. Eight out of ten books go nowhere and publishers know that. This is why I say without the fear of contradiction that the book is virtually dead the day the contract is signed.

But despite this reality, a lawyer can't do much for you. There have been, of course, many instances when books that were dead the day the contracts were signed went on to surprise everyone (especially the publisher) by becoming substantially successful books. All of this is again the result of too many books being published because the salesmen need something to sell and because the book publisher needs product to push into the bookstores.

If lawyers could correct all of this, I would be the first to cheer them on, but they are just another time-consuming roadblock—and an expensive one—that stands in the way of publishing books.

8

The Trouble with Editors

I once remarked to the president of a major book publishing company that as an experiment he should instruct his editors not to buy any books from literary agents for three months. The publisher smiled and agreed that it would be a good idea but, of course, he and I both knew that he would never do it.

Editors, for the most part, are wonderful—they are creative, concerned, interesting people with talent—but they can also be a little lazy, especially when it comes to dealing with agents. In a business where the acquisition of book properties can make or break not only the publishing firm but the editor, much too much dependence is put on the agent.

Most editors' idea of acquiring a book property is to have lunch or cocktails with an agent and to seek out the properties the agent is representing. For a young editor to get to meet with Sterling Lord, Henry Morrison, Scott Meredith or Morton Janklow is important because it means he will, he hopes, have the opportunity of bidding on one of the book properties represented by the superagents.

The truth is that if a young editor does get the chance to make an offer for one of the books represented by one of the major agents, it will probably be for a book he hasn't been able to unload. The "in" agents deal primarily with the "in" editors and publishers.

The bottom line is, of course, the fact that it is the literary agents who truly control book publishing and it is the editors (senior and junior) and the executives of publishing houses who live off what the agents offer their firms.

And that is the trouble with editors.

For too long, editors and publishers and virtually everybody else concerned with the acquisition of book properties have waited for the giant literary agents to either offer them a chance to buy one of their book properties or the opportunity to bid at an auction or multiple submission—knowing full well that they are in competition with other publishers.

No other business I know of is run successfully in this manner. It certainly violates all the principles of good business management taught at the Harvard Business School. If editors would only get out of their chairs and away from the lunches and cocktails and aggressively seek out properties themselves, then they and their firms and the industry itself would be more profitable and in better shape.

In all the years that I have gone after book properties—people or stories that I have either read about in magazines or newspapers or seen on television—I don't ever recall having any competition from an editor who was after the same property. And some of the book properties have been pretty obvious. They have in many instances been front page stories or personalities that were clearly major books.

In the mid-seventies Dr. Herbert Benson, director of the Hypertension Clinic at Boston's Beth Israel Hospital, had been conducting extensive research on the positive effects of meditation on the lowering of blood pressure. Benson's research and findings had not only been written about in leading medical journals but prominently reported in the *New York Times* as well. It was an obvious book.

I called Benson in Boston and was not at all surprised to find that despite all the publicity he had received (especially in the *New York Times* which is read by at least 75% of the editors in book publishing), I was the first to call. I visited Benson in Boston and a few days later I sold the book to Hillel Black and Larry Hughes at William Morrow for a modest advance of $20,000.

The book, titled *The Relaxation Response,* sold more than one million copies (in all editions) and was number one on the *New York Times* Best Sellers list for many months. The paperback rights were bought by Avon Books for $650,000. Bill Adler Books earned a profit in excess of $75,000 from that one phone call and quick trip to Boston.

The real point of the story is not the money we made or the fact that

William Morrow was lucky because we brought the book to them (and they had the good judgment to publish it) but rather all the other publishers, the Doubledays, the Simon & Schusters, the Random Houses and the like, who never even had the opportunity to publish *The Relaxation Response* because none of their editors even made a move (a phone call or a letter) to get the book property.

I wish I had $1,000 for every time an editor has asked me to make a call for him to try to get a book property. It is almost as if it is against the rules or the traditions of the business for an editor to go directly after a property. Needless to say, when an agent gets involved representing a book the price will probably be higher.

Larry King is the most successful radio talk show host in the country. His program is aired five nights a week from midnight to five A.M. on more than 225 stations over the Mutual Radio Network. Larry King is certainly well known to many in book publishing (especially the publicity and promotion people) since he interviews so many authors for his program and he is, in the vernacular of show business, "hot."

Yet, when I called Larry about writing a book I was once again the first to call, a fact I found astounding. Larry King was too obvious a choice for a book not to have heard from some editor.

I brought the Larry King book to Simon & Schuster where Michael Korda bought it for an advance of $50,000.

King is in the process of writing his book and if my guess has been correct then we, King and S & S will have a bestseller.

In many ways, many book editors are snobs. They seem to take pride in the fact that they really don't know what is going on television or, even worse, they have contempt for television and the people who are in front of the cameras.

This is a ridiculous attitude. You can't exist in book publishing today unless you watch television and know what is popular and what isn't. For that matter, you really can't function well in book publishing unless you read a good sampling of magazines, and I don't just mean *Time* or *Newsweek* or *Harper's*. I am referring to some of the women's magazines as well as mass appeal magazines like *People* and *Reader's Digest*.

By watching television and reading the popular magazines, editors would at least be aware of what the rest of the country is watching and reading. Most editors' idea of sampling television is watching public broadcasting.

When all is said and done, it is the editors who are the lifeblood of book publishing and unless they change their attitudes and habits, the growth and profitability of the industry will be seriously affected.

Not enough editors get deeply enough involved in book titles, jacket design and the promotion of the books they edit. That would never happen in the television or movie business. There the producers *are* involved in every aspect of the product from start to finish. The editor is in every sense of the word the producer of the book and should get involved all the way.

I don't believe that in the eighties publishing can exist with editors functioning for the most part as they have been for the last thirty years. It is time for a dramatic change.

This does not mean to say that there are not editors today who are first-rate—creative and aggressive when they have to be, wonderful at working with authors—and the kind of people who make publishing a joy.

Over the years, I have worked with many editors for whom I have respect and great affection. Perhaps the editor I have worked closest with over the years is Hillel Black at William Morrow.

Black, a former magazine editor (the old *Saturday Evening Post*) and the author of three published books, cares about books and about the authors with whom he works. Hillel will never win recognition as one of the ten best dressed men of the year and his taste usually runs to corduroy suits. Since I'm not known for my fashionable attire either, I must admit to a fondness in my heart for editors who don't put that much stock in what they wear.

Together with Hillel Black, Bill Adler Books has had many major bestsellers including *Harry S. Truman* by Margaret Truman, *The Relaxation Response* by Dr. Herbert Benson and *The Camera Never Blinks* by Dan Rather.

Black has also been the editor for Sidney Sheldon, Gail Sheehy and Tom Wicker, to mention but a few. He has a sense of humor and his judgment on a scale of one to ten would have to be an eight plus.

Hillel Black has one quality above all others that I think is important. He is willing to change his mind and listen to arguments.

One story that best illustrates this characteristic occurred only recently. I brought Hillel the first draft of a nonfiction book. He read the manuscript and was not impressed and rejected the book. Four months later, the author of the book was profiled in *Time* magazine in a very dramatic story. With the story from *Time* in hand, I went back to Hillel Black and Larry Hughes and told them that any author who could generate this kind of publicity without a press agent was worth reconsidering.

Black and Hughes did just that and the next day we had a contract for our author for $25,000. That takes class, style and good judgment. Editors who are locked into positions and don't move from them no matter what are not going to go very far.

The new editor-in-chief at Times Books, Jonathan Segal, is one of my favorite editors. Segal has a disarming sense of humor and talent. He was formerly a writer for the *New York Times* and senior editor at Simon & Schuster and Summit Books before he left to take over the editorial directorship of Times Books.

Segal gets deeply involved in the manuscripts he edits and I hope that with his editor-in-chief position at Times Books, he will be able to free himself from some of the day-to-day involvements which can, if an editor is not careful, take him away from acquisitions and the development of book properties.

Gene Brissie is the young, talented editor-in-chief of Cornerstone Library at Simon & Schuster. Brissie and I have done a lot of business together and I have found him in most cases to be intuitively correct and hard working and certainly an editor who has a great future ahead of him.

Ellis Amburn is one of the deans of book editors. Ellis has plied his trade at a number of publishing houses including Morrow and now Putnam's where he is the editorial director.

Ellis works especially well with celebrities and it was he who edited Shelley Winters's autobiography when he was at Morrow and, although I was not involved in that particular book, I am confident that only an editor with Ellis' patience and skills could have brought that book to its successful publication.

Ellis is the sort of editor who will call you frequently on the phone to prod and search for book properties and a phone call from Ellis Amburn can often begin with a line like, "What have you got for me?"

Roger Donald is the classy editor in charge of the New York office of the esteemed Boston publishing firm, Little, Brown. Although we have not done many books together, I have found on those occasions when Roger Donald was the editor on one of our properties that he had no hesitation at all in getting deeply involved in the publishing process. If anything, Roger Donald may get too involved but certainly the fact that he is concerned about the quality of his books is the reason I have to rank him as not only an asset to Little, Brown but to an industry desperately in need of editors who care.

If I were an editor looking for a place to work, some of the best publishing firms would have to be Alfred A. Knopf; William Morrow; Harper & Row; Random House; Atheneum; Farrar, Straus & Giroux and M. Evans.

Those companies rely heavily on the talents of their editors and give them the proper latitude for the development of book properties.

If I have one complaint about editors, it is that often they are too quick to reject a book. If a book is submitted to a publishing firm from an agent or an author with a track record, I think the editor owes it to himself and his publishing firm not to give a quick knee jerk reaction. Sometimes a book that seems like a terrible idea on Monday can be a first-rate idea by Thursday and the really smart editor will ponder the idea and its potential before accepting or rejecting the book. Many publishing firms have lost the chance to publish major book properties because their editors turned down the book instantaneously.

Women in Publishing

I'M sorry my daughter Diane has not selected book publishing as her career although I'm sure her field of urban studies is equally fascinating. I'm sorry because I can't think of another field that presents the opportunities offered to women that exist in book publishing.

Recently, Thelma Kandel, a writer I represent, published a book for The Linden Press titled *What Women Earn.* The Linden Press (a division of Simon & Schuster) is directed by Joni Evans who is one of the most successful women in publishing.

In *What Women Earn,* Thelma Kandel lists the women in book publishing who earn more than $100,000 a year. Those women are:

Sherry Arden, associate publisher, William Morrow & Co.

Joni Evans, publisher, The Linden Press

Joan Manley, publisher and chief executive officer, Time-Life Books

Mildred Marmur, subsidiary rights director, Random House

Helen Meyer, former president, Dell Publishing Co.

Beryl Robichaud, senior vice president, McGraw-Hill Book Co.

Patricia Wier, vice president, Encyclopaedia Britannica

Historically, book publishing has been a male-dominated business but now it has become a woman's business. Throughout the industry, there are women in major positions of responsibility and many of the power people in book publishing are women. The growth of women in book publishing has really taken place in the last five years and my hunch is that within the next ten years women will virtually dominate the industry.

Women have taken to book publishing in a big way for a number of reasons, but I think the primary one is that most books are bought by women and the industry finally came to the realization that if you were going to publish for women, it would make sense to have publishing decisions made by women.

Generalizations aren't fair, but it has been my experience that the women in book publishing—whether they are publishers, editors or agents—can be as tough, as ruthless, as devious and certainly as ambitious as their male counterparts.

In the course of any given business day, at least 60% of my phone calls or meetings are with women.

Who are the power women in book publishing and what are they really like?

It is only fair for me to discuss those women that I have personally dealt with. There are many I know only by name or reputation.

Sherry Arden has the title of vice president and associate publisher of William Morrow—a very important job—and she is also responsible for all subsidiary rights sales as well as publicity.

Sherry has the respect of Larry Hughes, the president and chief executive officer of Morrow, and her colleagues at William Morrow. Sherry Arden is bright and intuitive—two essential qualities for success in book publishing. Sherry also understands and is aware of the other media and she is able to quickly grasp the promotional potential of television. She has been through it many times before.

Joni Evans has come a long way quickly. Not yet forty, Joni Evans is president and publisher of The Linden Press, a subsidiary of Simon & Schuster.

Joni is married to Dick Snyder, the president of Simon & Schuster. On the surface it would appear like nepotism but nothing could be further from the truth. Joni Evans could work anywhere in book publishing at a salary equal to her six-figure income as publisher of The Linden Press.

Joni was rights director and associate publisher at Simon & Schuster and prior to that was a senior editor at William Morrow where she worked closely with Sherry Arden.

Joni is a brilliant editor and publishes her books with great enthusiasm and conviction.

Sherry Arden and Joni Evans are two of the best examples of the kinds of women in publishing. Both are happily married (Sherry has a daughter) and they are both aggressive and determined but by the same token remain feminine and appear to lead balanced lives.

Phyllis Grann is the publisher of G. P. Putnam's Sons. She is married to a doctor, has a family and if you didn't know she was one of the major personalities in book publishing, she could easily be taken for a happy suburban wife.

Phyllis Grann had been a senior editor at Simon & Schuster and for a very brief period of time was editor-in-chief at Pocket Books. I especially enjoy dealing with Phyllis because she gives you quick responses, even if they are negative, when you submit a book proposal to her.

Phyllis is a superb editor and her reputation as an editor and publisher of fiction is among the very best in book publishing.

Perhaps the most popular woman in book publishing is Joan Manley, the publisher and chief executive officer of Time-Life Books. As head of book publishing for Time, Inc., Joan Manley is responsible for Time-Life Books, Little, Brown, Book-of-the-Month Club and the New York Graphic Society.

I have never met Joan Manley but she has a reputation for being a no-nonsense executive who believes in the organization chart and the chain of command.

Before joining Time, Inc., Joan Manley was with Doubleday in their advertising department.

Some of the other powerful women in book publishing are:

Carole Baron, vice president and publisher, Dell Publishing Co.

Gladys Carr, editor-in-chief and chairman of the editorial board, McGraw-Hill Book Co.

Linda Grey, vice president and editor-in-chief, Bantam Books

Susan Kamil, vice president and director of subsidiary rights, Simon & Schuster

Elaine Koster, senior vice president and associate publisher, New American Library

Alice Mayhew, vice president and associate publisher, Simon & Schuster

Toni Morrison, senior editor, Random House

Betty Prashker, vice president and editor-in-chief, Crown Publishers

Eleanor Rawson, executive vice president, Rawson Associates

Grace Shaw, publisher, The Bobbs-Merrill Co.

Patricia Soliman, vice president and associate publisher, Simon & Schuster

Carol Southern, executive editor, Clarkson N. Potter

Nan Talese, vice president and executive editor, Houghton Mifflin Co.

Rena Wolner, vice president and publisher, Berkley Publishing Corp.

I do have a few observations about women in publishing.

They seem to have an advantage over men in book publishing when it comes to dealing with female authors and female agents. There is no question in my mind that among the many women in book publishing, a new girl network really does exist.

Women in book publishing are for the most part younger than their male counterparts. There are many women in book publishing who are in jobs of power under the age of thirty and even more between the ages of thirty and forty.

It has been my observation that women in book publishing are more aggressive and resourceful when it comes to securing acquisitions of book properties.

Two of the most powerful women in book publishing, Emily Boxer and Pat McMillen, don't work for publishing firms nor are they literary agents and yet they have a strong influence on which books will succeed and which books will not.

Emily Boxer is in charge of booking the authors who are to appear on the "Today" show and Pat McMillen is the senior producer for the "Donahue" show.

Emily Boxer knows the book business from the inside. Her background includes handling publicity for Simon & Schuster. Pat McMillen has been with the "Donahue" show since its inception and she knows and understands what books work for Donahue.

If Emily Boxer chooses your book for "Today" or if Pat McMillen books your author for "Donahue" you have at least a chance for a book that will sell well.

Myrna Blyth is the new editor-in-chief for *Ladies' Home Journal* and Myrna, along with Geraldine Rhoads who is the editor-in-chief of *Woman's Day*, are two of the most important people in the business of publishing books. If either one buys first serial rights to your book, it not only means extra money but it is a big boost for the book.

When you look at the prices paid for first serial rights, you can easily understand why women like Myrna Blyth, Geraldine Rhoads or Anne Smith, the new editor-in-chief of *Redbook*, have so much power. Not only can they enrich the pockets of authors, agents and publishers but by spending large sums of money for first serial rights, they can help to launch a book and do much toward its ultimate success.

Publishers find it invaluable to be able to tell the bookstores that a book they are publishing will be excerpted in a national magazine. It is superb promotion for the book since an excerpt in *Woman's Day* or *Ladies' Home Journal* reaches five to eight million readers.

The other major women's magazines (*Family Circle*, *Good Housekeeping* and *McCalls*) are edited by men.

I have known Gerry Rhoads for a long time since the days when we were both editors at *McCalls* magazine.

Myrna Blyth took over the editorship at *Ladies' Home Journal* when the *Journal*'s longtime editor, Lenore Hershey, became president of Charter Publishing Development, Inc.

Myrna is a bright woman—definitely out to succeed in propelling the *Journal* into the forefront of women's magazines. Prior to becoming editor-in-chief at *Ladies' Home Journal*, Myrna was fiction editor and then executive editor at *Family Circle* magazine.

First serial rights for books can be worth a lot of money. In the last few years there have been some substantial first serial sales:

Woman's Day paid $200,000 for Rose Kennedy's autobiography, *Times to Remember.*

Family Circle paid $100,000 for Lauren Bacall's autobiography, over $125,000 for five installments of Marjorie Craig's *10 Minute a Day Shape-up Program* and $75,000 for Richard Simmons's *Never Say Diet Cookbook.*

Ladies' Home Journal paid $120,000 for Betty Ford's autobiography, $100,000 for Sophia Loren's autobiography, $87,500 for Gail Sheehy's *Pathfinders* and about $100,000 for Kitty Kelley's book on Elizabeth Taylor.

Good Housekeeping paid between $60,000 and $100,000 for Martha Mitchell's autobiography, Eddie Fisher's autobiography, *The Complete Scarsdale Medical Diet* and *The Pritikin Diet* books.

There are many very successful literary agents who are women and they are among the most important people in the industry. Among the most powerful agents are Carol Brandt, Candida Donadio, Lucianne Goldberg, Elaine Markson, Gloria Safier, Rosalie Siegal, Erica Spellman at the William Morris Agency and Lynn Nesbit, Roberta Pryor and Esther Newberg, all at ICM.

There are other women who are up-and-coming editors who will be major factors in book publishing when many of the men who are now in power have retired and gone on to their condominiums and golf courses in Palm Springs. These young women will be making well over $100,000 a year in the future and they will control much of what America reads. Whether that is good or bad, we will find out as the years go by.

My own feeling is that the industry will change dramatically in the future because of these women who are not locked into the old ways of doing business and who seem to have a sense of what the public—especially women—want to read. And since women consist of 60 percent of the book buyers in the country, it stands to reason that the women in publishing should have a better understanding and sense about what women want to read.

Here are some of the up-and-coming young editors who I think will make their mark in book publishing in the future: Linda Cunningham at Bantam, Nancy Miller at Farrar, Straus & Giroux, Karen Solem, editor-in-chief of Silhouette Romances, Angela Miller at Simon & Schuster, Maria Guarnaschelli, Elizabeth Knappman and Pat Golbitz at William

Morrow, Barbara Lagowski at Bobbs-Merrill, Linda Cabasin and Diane Gedymin at M. Evans and Karen Van Westering at Doubleday.

In the not-too-distant future, Dick Snyder, Larry Hughes, and Bob Gottlieb will face stiff competition from these young women who know how to fight for what they want.

The future of book publishing belongs to them.

10

Book Packaging

I like to think that in a way Bill Adler Books has contributed to the development and growth of book packaging. Before the concept of book packaging was developed there were just the traditional agents—men and women who represented authors for the standard commission of 10%.

In the mid-sixties, Bill Adler Books, Inc. was set up to package books for publishers. We had a permanent editorial staff of five, including an editor-in-chief, and essentially we were in the business of contracting for and delivering completed manuscripts to publishers. We did not get involved in the actual production or printing of books because I have always felt that unless you really know the printing business, you could lose more than you could make.

As book packagers with a permanent editorial staff of bright, young people with excellent research backgrounds and writing skills, we were well equipped to deliver manuscripts to publishers on a variety of nonfiction subjects.

In the sixties, book publishers in the United States suddenly realized that they had published very little about the black experience in America just as book publishers in the seventies discovered they had published very little about the experiences of women.

Larry Hughes, the president of William Morrow, was one of the publishers who decided to correct the situation and publish more books about black Americans. One of the moves Larry made was to contract with Bill Adler Books on a retainer basis to develop books by and about black Americans.

It was a great assignment since there was so little that had been published up to that point that the creative opportunities were limitless. We hit the jackpot with the first book we packaged for Morrow. The book was called *Growing Up Black* and the author was Jay David (one of the pseudonyms we used for books packaged by us).

The book was an anthology of the best autobiographical writings by black Americans on what it was like to grow up black in white America. The book contained pieces going back to the Revolutionary War through to the present.

Hundreds of thousands of copies of *Growing Up Black* have been sold since its publication (in all editions) and we quickly followed up with *Growing Up African* and *Growing Up Jewish* (If a formula works, it pays to keep it going).

When we started packaging books we were paid an advance and a royalty by publishers just as if we were an author and out of the advances and royalties we had to pay our own editorial staff. We did, of course, own the copyrights for the books and in some instances (like *Growing Up Black*) we still receive royalties.

By 1970, we decided to change the direction of our packaging operation because I felt that a permanent editorial staff was unnecessary when we could use freelance writers and editors as we needed them. I never was crazy about permanent overhead since overhead usually forces you to take on projects that you don't have much faith in just to help pay for that overhead.

The idea of packaging books for publishers was really not very different from what producers had been doing in the television business—selling an idea or a proposal for a program or series to a network and then delivering the finished product. The producer would own the property and pay all the necessary costs required to produce the program. Since my early professional life had been spent in television, it was logical for me to adapt the principle of packaging books for publishers.

One of the most prolific book packagers over the years has been Lyle Kenyon Engel who has been enormously successful (and I assume has become very rich) packaging fiction series for paperback publishers.

Lyle Kenyon Engel's successful series have included *The Australians,*

Wagons West, Who's Who in Music and Records, the Nick Carter detective stories and the phenomenally successful eight-volume *Kent Family Chronicles* by John Jakes. The latest series, *Children of the Lion,* is based on the Bible.

Engel usually shares royalties and advances with his writers on a fifty-fifty basis. Engel dreams up the ideas, sells the property and then arranges for the books to be written.

Obviously, book packaging can be immensely profitable depending on how you structure the package and how much the packager has to pay the writer.

Many writers will work on a flat fee basis. They receive an outright payment from the packager for delivering a satisfactory manuscript but don't share in any of the royalty payments or subsidiary income received by the packager from the publisher.

This may seem unfair to the writer but actually there are many fine writers who are either between assignments or, worse, without any assignments who still have bills to pay and mortgage payments to meet and are more than happy to have the work.

The term used to describe these agreements is "writer for hire" and in many of the writer for hire or flat fee agreements (also referred to as a "buy out"), the writer does not receive credit as an author. Usually pseudonyms are used as in the case of Jay David or sometimes the name of the packager.

We have packaged hundreds of books and it has been a very lucrative part of our business. In many instances, we have shared a percentage of the royalties with the writer but it really depends on the individual situation.

Before you rush out to become a book packager you should be aware of some of the problems in packaging books. The biggest problem is the liability involved in contracting for a book for a specific advance payment and then having to deliver the manuscript for that advance.

If, for example, you sell a book idea for a $10,000 advance and you pay the writer a flat fee of $4,000 or $5,000 to write the book, you theoretically have a profit of $5,000 or $6,000 plus whatever profit you may make from royalties. But what happens if the writer for hire does not deliver an acceptable manuscript and you then have to hire another writer?

Book packaging can be treacherous unless you are sure of the writers who work with you and unless you are able to structure a good deal for yourself with the publisher.

In a sense, the book packager is not unlike the publisher. He risks his money for a book to be written because even though the money has been advanced by the publisher, it is, like most advances, fully returnable if the manuscript is not acceptable.

A perfect example of the kinds of book packages that have been profitable for us involves a book we just completed for M. Evans. I suggested to Herb Katz, the editor-in-chief at M. Evans, a book based on some research that I had read about on a recent trip to Paris.

I had learned that a French doctor along with a doctor in Canada had conducted successful research with pregnant women on how certain kinds of diets could increase the chances of the selection of the sex of a child.

Katz immediately grasped the potential of the idea and a few days after I proposed the book, M. Evans signed a contract with us for an advance of $15,000 for a book titled *The Pre-Conception Diet*. We quickly made an agreement with Bill Proctor, an excellent writer we have represented, to research and write the book on a fifty-fifty basis.

Even if *The Pre-Conception Diet* doesn't earn any royalties beyond its advance, we will have made a profit of $7,500 and Proctor will have been paid $7,500 for writing the book. Proctor, for his part, was as convinced as I was (and as Herb Katz was) that the book would earn substantially more than $7,500, so he was willing to gamble that his 50% would eventually be well worth his efforts.

Many more entrepreneurs in book publishing are turning to book packaging and I'm sure that soon there will be almost as many book packagers as there are traditional agents. If you are creative and really enjoy getting involved in developing book ideas and manuscripts, then book packaging can be very rewarding.

11

The Title on the Jacket

IF the quality of the manuscript is important in book publishing then the title of the book is equally important. A good, strong, selling title can make or break a book.

When Dr. Herbert Benson finished the manuscript for his book, most of the people at William Morrow wanted to title it *The R Response*. Benson objected. He believed that *The R Response* was too gimmicky and didn't properly describe the book. He wanted to call the book *The Relaxation Response*. Benson won and I believe that the title played a part in the book becoming the number one bestseller the year it was published.

Fortunately for authors, publishers have within the last few years been paying more attention to titles (as movie people have been doing for years). I have even sold books recently based on the title alone.

One recent example was a book we just sold to M. Evans titled *How to Help Your Man Succeed*. As soon as Herb Katz heard the title he said, "That's really a great title. We should be able to make that into a bestselling book."

For a book title to succeed, it must do a number of things.

- It must adequately describe the book.
- It should attract attention. With 30,000 hardcover books pub-

lished every year you need a book title that will stand out of the crowd.

- The title shouldn't be too long. *War and Peace* is only three words but it said it all.

  When it came time to select the title for Howard Cosell's first book it was obvious to me that the best title for Cosell's autobiography was one word—*Cosell*. That started a trend and now many celebrity autobiographies have one-word titles like *Cavett* and *Donahue* and *Nancy* (Nancy Reagan's book).

- The right title for a book is as important in fiction as it is in nonfiction.

  Valley of the Dolls was the perfect title for Jacqueline Susann's all time bestseller because "dolls" was the word used to describe the pills taken by the Hollywood crowd.

- Sometimes the wrong title can effectively diminish the potential for a book if the title is too confusing and says nothing.

I have often thought that before the title is selected for a book, an ad should be written to see how the title can be described when it is advertised. The title is not any different from the headline or advertising slogan used by the ad agencies to promote a product. If the headline doesn't work, then the sales of the product will be negatively affected.

Some of the most successful entrepreneurs in book publishing, such as Robert Ringer, place heavy emphasis on the book title. Ringer, author of the bestselling *Looking Out for No. 1*, also packaged or published bestselling books with such merchandisable titles as: *Living Alone and Liking It*, *Crisis Investing*, *Nice Girls Do* and *The Alpha Strategy*.

Directness is an important asset for a title that will work.

In 1968 a young advertising executive by the name of Eric Weber had an idea for a book and, since he was an advertising copy writer, he knew that the title for his book had to convey the theme of the book quickly and directly. The title of the book was *How to Pick Up Girls;* that title certainly leaves little doubt as to what the book is about.

How to Pick Up Girls has been an enormous success since it was first published in 1970 and has sold more than 650,000 copies. It was originally published by Weber's own direct mail publishing firm, Symphony Press.

Certainly one of the all time bestselling nonfiction books has been Dale Carnegie's *How to Win Friends and Influence People*. There is no gray area with that title. It is clear and tells you exactly what the book says. If Dale Carnegie had used a more obtuse title like *Friendship and Other Relations with People,* I doubt if the book would still be earning royalties thirty-three years later.

A good title can't make a bad book into a bestseller but a good book with a bad title will have a difficult time in the bookstores.

Some recent books that I thought had titles that were not very good were:

The Charisma Book by Doe Lang. An excellent book about how you can improve your personal charm and charisma but the title sounds as if it were an anthology. That book could have done much better with a more dramatic and enticing title.

Harvard Medical School Health Letter. This book showed great promise when it was published since it was the first general publication from the prestigious Harvard Medical School *Health Letter,* but to title a book like that for the general public was a mistake. The book certainly should have had a more commercial title and perhaps could have been a bestseller if it had.

Titles for books should not just describe the book but should offer some sort of promise or reason to spend ten or twelve dollars to buy it. This is especially true in nonfiction.

Confession and Avoidance by Leon Jaworski. This memoir by the famed Watergate prosecutor is the worst title I can think of, and I'm still trying to find out what the word "avoidance" means.

Mother's Medicine by Nancy Moore Thurmond. Senator Strom Thurmond's wife had been writing a successful newspaper column for a South Carolina newspaper on raising children when I approached her to do a book based on her column. The column was titled "Mother's Medicine" but the book should not have been. What we forget about newspaper columns is that the titles come free with the newspaper. But for a book to work, the title must be stronger and more descriptive; in this case it wasn't.

Self-Portrait by Gene Tierney. A poignant book about the Hollywood star but a very unexciting title. *Self-Portrait* is too static and not dramatic enough.

The Art of Living by John Cameron Swayze. Again, a much overused title and if I never represent a book again with the words "the art of" in the title, I will be very happy.

One of the best titles for a book published recently was *How to Negotiate Anything* by Herb Cohen. I don't know if Herb Cohen or his publisher, Lyle Stuart, came up with that title, but it was inspired.

Herb Cohen is one of the country's foremost experts on negotiation, and he lectures around the country before business groups and government agencies on successful negotiation. The title for his book was right on the money—no confusion about the content of the book and that last word of the title, "anything," said that this was a book for everybody.

Cohen's book has sold more than 220,000 copies and has been on the *New York Times* Best Sellers list for more than 35 weeks.

If you are going to write a book (especially nonfiction), it is a good idea to think of a strong selling title before you submit the finished manuscript to the publisher. You can't always rely on the publisher to come up with the best title. Remember the publisher is concerned with hundreds of books every year but you are only concerned with one—yours!

Throughout this book I have tried (and I hope successfully) to get across the point that the one who succeeds is the one who does not take anything for granted—especially when it comes to one's publisher, and that means everything from the title of the book to the advertising and promotion. Get involved!

No chapter about book titles would be complete without a sampling of some of the book titles that I've admired and that certainly have been successful.

Pills That Don't Work by Dr. Sidney Wolfe. A strong, descriptive title that clearly defines the book.

Color Me Beautiful by Carol Jackson. A perfect title for a book on beauty tips for women.

The Sky's the Limit by Wayne Dyer. A first-rate inspirational title.

How to Make Love to a Man by Alexandra Penney. No wonder this book is a bestseller. The title offers the promise in clear language.

Living Alone and Liking It by Lynn Shahan. No confusion about this book. It says to people who are living alone that it can be joyful and pleasurable.

It Sure Looks Different from the Inside by Ron Nessen. Nessen's book about his experiences as President Ford's press secretary had one of the best titles in a long time. The title described exactly what Nessen was writing about. He was telling the story of how different it is working inside the White House rather than covering the White House as a news correspondent.

The Camera Never Blinks by Dan Rather with Mickey Herskowitz. No one will be able to come up with a better title for a broadcast journalist than this one.

12

My Biggest Mistakes in Publishing

SOMEBODY had suggested that Judy Mazel contact me. She called from California and said she wanted to write a book called *The Beverly Hills Diet.*

This was shortly after the enormous success of *The Scarsdale Diet,* and I thought that even if Judy Mazel was a legitimate diet expert and her diet did work, her idea sounded too much like a ripoff of Dr. Tarnower's book.

Ms. Mazel sounded very positive over the phone and would definitely have to be described as a person who sells hard. Hard sells usually turn me off but in this case I suggested to Judy Mazel that she send me the materials she had prepared for her book.

A few days later I received in the mail a proposal for a diet as well as substantial publicity materials—newspaper and magazine stories about Judy Mazel. I glanced at the diet and was not impressed. It seemed to me to be a one-gimmick diet and, although Ms. Mazel's publicity related mostly to her diet school in Beverly Hills, I was still skeptical.

I have always felt that a good agent should be selective in what he submits to publishers and should certainly not send to publishers every book proposal that comes across his desk. If an agent sends out too many proposals for books that obviously won't work, he will quickly diminish his effectiveness and his book proposals will receive the attention they deserve—very little.

In the case of *The Beverly Hills Diet,* I decided to think about it and wait a week before making up my mind. During the course of that week, Judy Mazel called every day and it was clear to me that this was a very impatient lady. She was beginning to annoy me. After about the sixth phone call, I decided that Judy Mazel and *The Beverly Hills Diet* were not for me.

The rest, of course, is publishing history. Macmillan went on to publish the book and it has been one of the all time bestselling diet books.

Do I regret the decision? Yes and no.

Yes, because representing *The Beverly Hills Diet* and Judy Mazel would have been worth well over $100,000 to us in commissions alone but no, because I still believe *The Beverly Hills Diet* is a gimmick and not really a sound diet.

About seven years ago, I received a phone call from the now super-agent Morton Janklow asking me if I would like to represent a novel. At the time, Janklow was primarily practicing law although he was representing a few writers like William Safire.

Janklow indicated over the phone that since he really wasn't representing much fiction that perhaps I could take on the project.

"It's a novel about the CIA," Janklow told me, "written by somebody who really knows a lot about the CIA and how it works."

"Who's the author?" I asked Janklow.

"John Ehrlichman," he replied.

I was a little surprised. Ehrlichman was at the time on trial for the break-in at Daniel Ellsberg's psychiatrist's office and, of course, he had recently resigned as assistant to the president in the wake of the Watergate scandal.

"Ehrlichman is very anxious to have the novel sold quickly," Janklow told me. I agreed to read the manuscript overnight, and he messengered a copy over to me.

I read the novel and although I was not overly impressed, I thought that it was pretty good for a first novel. It certainly sounded authentic in its description of the CIA. I decided, however, that before I gave Janklow or Ehrlichman an answer, I would call some of the more important editors in town to see how they felt about a novel by John Ehrlichman since sentiment within the publishing community at the time was very anti-Nixon, to say the least. I spoke to at least ten editors at the ten major publishing firms and none of them was interested in even looking at a novel written by John Ehrlichman.

One of the editors who wasn't interested was Jonathan Dolger (now an agent) who was at the time managing editor at Simon & Schuster. Jonathan, not unlike the other editors I talked to, thought it was a terrible idea.

I informed Janklow and Ehrlichman personally that I didn't want to represent the book.

A few months later, I was in London with my wife, Gloria, on business and there in an issue of the international edition of the *Herald Tribune* was a picture of John Ehrlichman with Richard Snyder taken shortly after Ehrlichman had signed a contract with Simon & Schuster for the publication of his novel.

After I had turned down the chance to represent Ehrlichman's novel, Janklow finally decided to represent the book himself and submitted it to Michael Korda at Simon & Schuster.

Ehrlichman's novel, *The Company*, went on to be a major bestseller and was even sold to NBC as a television miniseries.

Incidentally, it is not unusual for one editor at a publishing firm to reject a book only to have the same book accepted by another editor.

I first met Barbara Howar at a dinner party at William Safire's Washington home a number of years ago. Barbara was well known in Washington as a television interviewer and as part of Washington's "in" crowd. She was frequently mentioned in the "Eye" column in *Womens Wear Daily* which I always read for book ideas.

I found Barbara Howar to be attractive, vivacious and witty. I knew immediately that she would be a promotable and potentially bestselling author.

One incident at the Safire dinner convinced me to do a book with Barbara. After dinner, Safire suggested to his dinner guests that the men go into one room of his spacious home for cigars and brandy while the women were directed into another room. (In all fairness to Safire, I have to say that the dinner took place almost ten years ago.) Barbara Howar would not hear of it. If the men were going into a separate room for brandy so was Barbara.

When I returned to New York, I called Barbara and asked her if she would be interested in writing a book about the people and events in Washington. She was.

A few weeks later, I invited Barbara to lunch with a number of editors. One was Sandy Richardson, then the editor-in-chief at Doubleday, and the other was Hillel Black, then senior editor and now editor-in-chief at Morrow. Both Black and Richardson expressed strong interest in doing a book with Barbara. They asked for an outline and Barbara said she would write one.

I was never able to get an outline out of Barbara and I eventually lost interest in pursuing her for a book.

Barbara Howar's book was finally published and was represented by Sterling Lord. Barbara's first book (the one I suggested she write) was a major bestseller. It was titled *Laughing All the Way.*

The Barbara Howar experience taught me a lesson I have heeded ever since: When you have a book property that has bestseller potential, don't wait for an outline. Somehow you must get the book contract.

Actually that is sound advice for not only agents but for publishers because had either Sandy Richardson or Hillel Black offered Barbara Howar a contract without an outline they would have had a bestseller.

Sometimes a bestseller can be right in front of your eyes and you may not see it.

Barbara Gordon was an NBC television producer I had known casually when I worked at NBC. Barbara had produced a documentary about a courageous woman who had been the mayor of a city in New Jersey who knew she was dying of cancer and yet carried on her life despite her terminal and painful illness.

Barbara was to collaborate with Barbara Lang, a writer I represented, on a book about this brave woman to be published by Playboy Press.

Looking back now I should have realized that Barbara Gordon's behavior was at times a little unusual. She frequently arrived late for meetings and occasionally missed meetings altogether.

Barbara never did write the book for me, but she did go on with another agent to write the bestselling book about her experiences with Valium called *I'm Dancing as Fast as I Can.*

There have been other books that have slipped through my fingers for one reason or another, and I hope I have learned—but probably not.

I'm sure I will still turn down authors like Judy Mazel who press too hard or novelists like John Ehrlichman who don't seem to interest the publishers.

In dollars and cents, books I have lost or rejected have easily cost me $250,000 in commissions.

13

Publishing Stories I've Never Told Before

THE idea for *The Kennedy Wit* came to me shortly after John F. Kennedy became president. It was obvious to me that Kennedy was a man of great style, charm and wit. I decided to put together a collection of Kennedy's best witticisms from his speeches, press conferences and the like.

A number of publishers turned down the book but finally Scott Meredith, my agent at the time, was able to sell the book to Bennett Cerf at Random House with Dell purchasing the paperback rights.

Just before Random House signed the contract, Cerf asked one of his editors to check with Pierre Salinger, Kennedy's press secretary, to see if the White House had any objection to a book called *The Kennedy Wit.* This was, I thought, an unnecessary step since the president's remarks and speeches were all in the public domain, as is the case with all public figures.

However, Bennett Cerf wanted to maintain good relations with the Kennedy White House figuring, I guess, that he might publish Kennedy's memoirs someday. And Jacqueline Kennedy had just conducted her famous televised tour of the White House and all the major publishers were after the book rights.

Salinger checked the Random House request out with Ted Sorenson, the assistant to the president and Kennedy's primary phrasemaker.

Neither Salinger nor Sorenson had any objection to the book. It was a "go" situation. The contracts were signed and the manuscript was quickly completed and ready to go to the printers.

The book was already in galleys when Pierre Salinger mentioned to the president that Random House was going to publish a book called *The Kennedy Wit.* Obviously, this was the first time that Kennedy had heard about the book. He was furious and he quickly made it clear to Salinger that he didn't want the book published.

We live in a democracy. Because the president of the United States doesn't want a book published should mean nothing if the publisher wants to exercise his first amendment right to publish what he wants—when he wants.

Salinger called Bennett Cerf directly and told him that the president would prefer that Random House not publish *The Kennedy Wit.*

To put this story in historical perspective, I should say that Kennedy learned of the impending publication of the book shortly after the Bay of Pigs disaster and obviously didn't feel that the time was right for a book to be published about his humor.

Bennett Cerf told Salinger they would not publish the book and informed me, that as far as Random House was concerned, the book was dead. Dell immediately withdrew their contract for the paperback rights and I was left with a manuscript and no publisher.

Had this incident taken place during the Nixon years I am confident that the story of a president putting pressure on a publisher not to publish a book would have had serious repercussions. But Kennedy in the early sixties could do no wrong (despite the Bay of Pigs), and he and Mrs. Kennedy were the most popular first family with the media—including book publishers.

I tried to sell *The Kennedy Wit* to every other publisher in town but for one reason or another I was turned down. Some publishers just didn't like the manuscript. Others didn't want to cross the White House. Some were still hoping to get the book rights to Mrs. Kennedy's tour of the White House. The book was published and didn't sell very well anyway.

Another factor that I discovered later from conversations with publishers was Bobby Kennedy. Many of the publishers didn't want to upset the attorney general by publishing a book his brother didn't want published.

But whatever the reasons, the White House effectively killed any opportunity for me to have *The Kennedy Wit* published.

Shortly after the tragic events in Dallas, I again tried to have the book published, but this time Random House, Dell and a host of other publishers turned it down because they thought it was in bad taste and they didn't believe Americans wanted to remember their slain president with a book called *The Kennedy Wit.*

I finally found a small but smart publisher, Citadel Press, to publish the book. *The Kennedy Wit* became a major bestseller and was on the *New York Times* Best Sellers list for six months.

A short postscript to this story occurred a few years ago when I received a phone call from Patricia Kennedy Lawford, President Kennedy's sister. It was just before Christmas and Mrs. Lawford wanted to know if I had any extra copies of *The Kennedy Wit* that she could give to some of her nieces and nephews as gifts. (The book was by this time out of print and not available in bookstores.)

William Safire is an old friend. The successful author and *New York Times* columnist and I both started our careers together with the popular "Tex and Jinx" radio and television programs at NBC in the early fifties. We maintained our friendship over the years and although Bill had his attorney and old friend, Morton Janklow, represent his book deals, Bill and I saw each other often and frequently talked about books.

One day in 1974 Bill and I were eating lunch in my office. Halfway through a pastrami sandwich Safire mentioned that he would like to write his first novel.

"Why don't you go ahead and write a novel, Bill?," I asked him.

"Frankly," Safire replied, "I don't have an idea for one. You're an idea man. Why don't you come up with an idea for a novel for me?"

"I'll be glad to, Bill, but even though we're old friends I'm going to have to charge you. Developing ideas is part of my business."

"How much do you want?" Safire asked in his usual direct manner.

"If you write a novel based on an idea that I develop for you, Bill, then I want 10%," I replied.

"That's fine," Safire said, "but Janklow will have to represent the deal as my agent and I'll be paying him 10% as well."

It was five minutes later that I came up with the idea for a novel to take place in Washington, D.C. about a president who went blind. His blindness tested the Twenty-Fifth Amendment to the Constitution which deals with presidential disability.

Safire immediately sparked to the idea and in what seemed like a very short period of time wrote an outline and a sample chapter for the novel, which he titled *Full Disclosure.*

The book was bought by Doubleday for $25,000 and a few days after Doubleday had made an offer Safire called me. "With an advance of $25,000," Bill said, "I really can't afford to pay you 10% and Janklow 10%. There isn't enough left to make it worthwhile for me to write the book."

"Why don't you cut it in half, Bill?," I suggested. "Instead of 20%, Janklow and I will split 10%."

Safire was pleased. Janklow agreed and Bill went on to write his novel.

In 1976 Safire finished *Full Disclosure* and submitted it to his editor at Doubleday, Sandy Richardson. Richardson was enthusiastic about the novel and quickly thereafter a publishing phenomenon occurred.

The Literary Guild and the Book-of-the-Month Club entered into a bidding war for the rights to Safire's novel. The Literary Guild won out with an offer of $275,000, an unheard-of price for a first novel.

The book was still in manuscript form when the paperback publishers decided to get into the act and in short order, after a spirited auction, Ballantine Books bought the reprint rights for $1,350,000—the highest price ever paid by a paperback house for a first novel.

That little idea born over a pastrami sandwich at my desk was now a major profit center. I was elated not just for Safire but because I was involved—if only as the father of the idea.

It was a few days later that my elation was tempered by the realization that the 5% I had given back to Safire was now worth a considerable amount of money. I called Safire in Washington and told him I wanted to see him the next time he was in New York. We agreed to meet early the next week for a drink at the Four Seasons.

Bill knew what I wanted to talk about and, as usual, he came straight to the point.

"Let's make it 7½% for you and 7½% for Janklow," Safire suggested.

"It's a deal," I replied quickly.

That extra 2½% was equal to an additional $15,000, and I thought that a fair solution had been arrived at. Safire is still a friend and he is now writing a new novel for which he did not come to me for the idea.

Developing ideas for writers—even writers who are represented by other agents—has always been a lucrative and productive business for me. That part of my business started at a dinner with my then agent, Scott Meredith, at Sardi's restaurant.

"You know," I told Scott during dinner, "my real strength comes from the development of ideas. Obviously, I can't write all the books for which I have ideas nor do I have the talent to write all of them."

"Well," Scott said, "I don't think that a first-rate writer is going to pay for using somebody else's idea. Writers like to write books based on their own ideas. It just isn't done."

I let Meredith finish and then told him that even if that were the case I had an idea for a book that I thought could make a lot of money. I could tell Scott was just being polite when he asked me what the idea was.

"It's a book about Joe Kennedy, Jr.," I continued. "It's the story of John F. Kennedy's older brother who was killed during World War II—the son Joe Kennedy, Sr. had hoped would someday be the first Catholic president of the United States."

Scott's eyes lit up and he reacted instantaneously. "That's a great idea," he said, "and I have the perfect writer."

The writer was Hank Searls, the book was *The Lost Prince*, and for everybody concerned it was a financial success. Recently *The Lost Prince* was made into a movie for television.

That dinner at Sardi's with Scott Meredith opened a whole new avenue of producing revenue for Bill Adler Books. Not only did we have a percentage for coming up with the idea for *The Lost Prince* but we have developed more than 100 books for other writers over the last few years alone. I believe we were the first to work in this manner—where we just developed the idea and someone else wrote the book, and we were paid for developing the concept for the book.

I have often been asked if anyone has ever taken one of my ideas without compensating me. As surprising as it may seem, that has only happened once. Most people don't steal ideas, but more importantly an idea has to be executed; so taking the idea doesn't mean much unless you have the talent to do something with it.

That one time, however, occurred with a writer I had been representing. For legal reasons, I'll call the writer Mark Paul. (Obviously, that is not his name.)

Mark Paul had been a relatively well-known writer before he wrote his first novel which I represented and for the purpose of this story am calling *The Train.*

The Train was published in hardcover by a major publisher and was also published in paperback. It was mildly successful.

I also represented Mark Paul's second novel which has been completed but not yet published.

After Mark Paul's second novel had been sold, he was searching for an idea for his third novel. He had decided to write a novel about a woman who becomes a successful executive and how it affects her life. Mark Paul and I met with the editor of his previous novels to discuss the idea. The editor did not like the idea that Paul had presented for his third novel, so at the meeting I suggested instead that he write a novel about a woman who succeeds in show business against the background of Hollywood.

The editor sparked to my idea immediately and so did Mark Paul, who agreed to do an outline based on my idea. When the outline was completed, the editor, even though he had liked the original idea, decided not to make an offer for the book.

A few weeks later, I received a letter from Mark Paul saying that he had decided to use another agent but that he would, of course, compensate me for my idea.

I forgot about Mark Paul (not difficult to do) and my idea until nine months later when I was having dinner with the president of the paperback publishing firm that had published Paul's first novel.

"What ever happened to Mark Paul?" I asked the publisher.

"Haven't you heard?" he said. "His novel about a woman in show business was sold to another paperback house for a lot of money."

It was nice to know that at least my idea had found a home.

I called Mark Paul and asked him where my percentage was for developing the idea for his new novel. He promised to get back to me within a week. He never did, and I decided to send an official letter to his new publisher notifying them that the novel by Mark Paul they had under contract was based on my idea for which I had not been compensated.

Within two weeks, Mark Paul sued me for one million dollars for writing that letter to his new publisher. The suit was eventually dropped by Mark Paul but it cost me $2,500 in legal fees. Not only was I out one good idea for a novel but I had lost some money to boot.

As of the writing of this book, Paul's novel, based on my idea, has yet to be published.

It was my one and only experience with an idea that drifted out of my hands.

Joanne Carson was Johnny Carson's second wife. (Carson has been married three times.) Joanne, a former airline stewardess, is thin, pretty and tense. I met her through a friend in California where she was still living after her divorce from Carson.

No one who had ever been close to Carson had written about him, and when I heard that Joanne Carson wanted to write a book, I jumped at the chance to meet with her on my next trip to California.

I had dinner with Joanne Carson and her boyfriend at the Beverly Wilshire Hotel where we talked about her book. Joanne told me that the book she wanted to write was mainly about her interest in health, nutrition and related areas, but that she would be willing to include some of her life with Johnny in the book. "Even if you only write a couple of chapters about Carson," I told his ex-wife, "the book will be a bestseller."

Toward the end of our pleasant dinner meeting, Joanne Carson mentioned that she would be visiting New York in a few weeks and asked if I knew of a limousine service that she could use while she was in the city.

I volunteered the services of the limousine service that I used and told Joanne that the car would meet her at the airport and be available whenever she needed it in New York. I also arranged for her to get tickets to *Dancin'*, the hit Broadway show she indicated she would like to see.

My investment in a possible bestseller was a dinner for three at the Beverly Wilshire Hotel, two tickets to a Broadway show and the use of a limousine. It seemed like a reasonable investment for a few first-person chapters by someone who had been married to Johnny Carson.

I didn't calculate that two things would happen.

The first was that Mrs. Carson would use that limousine extensively when she was in Manhattan, and the second was that I would hear from Joanne shortly after her return to California to tell me that she had just checked her divorce settlement with Johnny and she would stand the chance of losing her alimony if she wrote anything about him that might hold Carson up to ridicule or cause him embarrassment.

In all fairness to Joanne Carson, I believe she was well meaning in her desire to write her book but got nervous after she checked with her attorney or reread her divorce settlement.

So much for my book which would reveal for the first time what the real Johnny Carson was like.

Through a mutual friend, I met Steve Allen who turned out to be by far the most prolific writer of books I have ever encountered. I don't even recall the title of the first book idea we developed for the man who for so many years was the witty host of the "Tonight" program, but I do know that in the course of about two years I developed and sold four books for Steve, all of which he has written or is in the process of finishing.

Allen must keep his secretaries typing around the clock because he usually dictates into a small recorder that he carries with him wherever he goes. Allen's secretaries then transcribe what he has dictated.

How he is able to write several books at the same time continues to amaze me. What is even more amazing is that the quality and imagination of his writing is first-rate.

Despite the fact that I have sold four books for Steve Allen, I have met him only once. That was briefly for a cup of coffee at the famous "21" Club in New York, and that meeting almost didn't take place.

Allen was having lunch at "21" and I was having lunch at the Four Seasons. I had agreed to meet him at "21" after my lunch.

I dashed over to "21" but was barred at the door.

"I'm sorry, sir," the gentleman told me, "you can't come in."

"What's wrong?" I asked.

"No tie," I was told. "We require a tie at '21.' "

"I'm here to see Steve Allen," I defiantly told the obstinate man at the door.

I am sure he was convinced that considering the way I was dressed (no tie, seersucker jacket and khaki pants—it was summertime) that I couldn't possibly be there to see one of America's great television personalities.

"I'll have to check," he told me.

A few minutes later (it seemed like an hour), he returned and was more cordial than he had been before.

"Steve is upstairs in the dining room," the man at the door told me, "but I'm afraid you will have to put this on before you go up there."

He handed me a ratty, shopworn clip-on bow tie which I struggled to put on as I went up the stairs for my first and only meeting with Steve Allen. But I almost lost four books because of a tie.

John DeLorean never really wanted to write his book. I should have sensed that after my first meeting with him. He was charming, articulate and obviously concerned with image.

Today, John DeLorean is the founder and president of DeLorean Motor Company, which may well become the only new automobile company to succeed since the Chrysler Company was founded.

DeLorean, when we first met in his attractive and handsomely appointed offices in Detroit, had just started his own consulting firm after resigning from General Motors where he had risen to executive vice president and where he was considered the maverick of the auto industry.

"I want to tell it like it is," DeLorean told me and Pat Wright, the then automobile editor for *Business Week* magazine. "Nobody would believe what goes on on the fortieth floor where the top executives at GM have their offices."

Pat Wright, DeLorean and I decided then and there to call the book *On a Clear Day You Can See General Motors,* a title that best described the honest, straightforward portrait of the largest auto company in American history that DeLorean intended to write with the assistance of Pat Wright.

At the time of this first meeting with DeLorean, I was the executive editor of Playboy Press and the DeLorean book was one I had acquired for them. Even DeLorean's agreement to write his book for Playboy revealed something about the man. Most major corporation executives would have preferred to be published by Harper & Row, Simon & Schuster, Doubleday or Random House—a publishing company more in the mainstream. But Playboy suited DeLorean.

Even in the beginning, DeLorean's motives for wanting to "tell all" about the auto industry were not clear to me. Was it ego? Money? Revenge? Or was it because he wanted more people to know what really happened in the upper strata of America's corporate life?

Wright and DeLorean began to work *On a Clear Day You Can See General Motors* almost immediately and for the first five or six months everything went smoothly. But then rumblings began and the signs from Detroit and DeLorean were not good.

It was at this time that DeLorean was beginning to talk seriously about starting his own automobile company which seemed like an impossible dream. He began to have second thoughts about certain sections in the manuscript and he expressed his concern to Pat Wright and me that perhaps he was coming down too hard on the corporate executives on the fortieth floor.

Behind DeLorean's concern was the fact that he, more than anything else, wanted his own motor company and anything that was going to keep him from that dream was a problem.

Pat Wright kept writing and making changes and softening certain sections of the book, and I kept assuring DeLorean at numerous meetings in New York and Detroit that the book would only help his future aspirations. "It will attract attention to you as a man and a leader of industry," I kept repeating.

DeLorean kept agreeing and assuring both Pat and me that he wanted to do the book, but as DeLorean's plans for the DeLorean Motor Company began to take shape, it became obvious that the book was not his first priority.

Pat Wright kept working and finally finished the book and submitted the manuscript to me (as his editor) for approval. "It's great, Pat," I told him.

A copy of the manuscript went to DeLorean and Playboy Press announced *On a Clear Day You Can See General Motors* with a full-page ad in its catalog. Playboy even announced the book in a full-page ad in *Publishers Weekly* and the salesmen started selling the book to the bookstores.

The advance orders from the stores were sensational and it looked as though we were going to have a major bestseller. It was then that DeLorean said he wanted to make changes in the manuscript.

"Nothing major," DeLorean assured Pat Wright and me. "It shouldn't take long to fix up the manuscript."

It did take long and DeLorean kept procrastinating with Pat Wright getting more and more annoyed. Wright had, after all, spent one year writing the book.

Playboy Press, for its part, kept trying to convince DeLorean that the book should be published and that if we delayed much longer it would mean that all the bookstores would cancel their orders, and we would have to recatalog the book and sell it all over again.

DeLorean was unavailable or out of town or busy but finally at a showdown meeting in New York, DeLorean told Pat Wright and me that he needed a little bit more time but after that he would be ready to go ahead. From what he told us at the meeting, it was clear that DeLorean was particularly concerned at the kind of pressure General Motors might put on car dealers when the DeLorean car was eventually distributed. "GM is very powerful," DeLorean said, "and I don't want them to be so mad at my book that they'll make it almost impossible for me to get any dealers to handle my car."

The New York meeting only led to more delay and, although the book had been reannounced for the next season and resold by the salesmen to the bookstores, DeLorean refused to give his okay for the book and so notified Playboy in writing.

By this time I was no longer at Playboy and Mike Cohn, the director of the book division, had left as well. Everybody gave up on the DeLorean book except one person. And that person was Pat Wright.

Pat Wright made up his mind to publish the DeLorean book himself—without John DeLorean's permission. It was a gutsy thing to do. First of all, Wright had to raise the money to publish the book, which he did. He then had to find a distributor for the book, which he did—Caroline House—and then he had to be prepared for what could be a substantial lawsuit from John DeLorean.

But Wright went ahead and the book was published. It was more than just published. *On a Clear Day You Can See General Motors* was a smash hit and was on the *New York Times* Best Sellers list for many weeks. The paperback rights alone went for $250,000 to Avon and out of the ashes and difficulties of more than three years, Pat Wright not only had the DeLorean book published but he made a substantial—very substantial—profit.

As for DeLorean, he made some noises about suing, claiming that the book was unauthorized, but he never did. My guess is that DeLorean was finally pleased with the book and proud that it was such a bestseller.

It took a long time in getting there and certainly the saga of *On a Clear Day You Can See General Motors* is one of the most unusual in book publishing.

Shortly after John F. Kennedy became president, I read an article about him in the *Saturday Evening Post.* In the article it mentioned that Kennedy received more mail than any president in recent memory and that he especially received an enormous amount of mail from young people. It was then while reading that article that I got the idea for what was to be one of my most successful books—*Kids' Letters to President Kennedy.*

My biggest problem once I got the idea was how to get permission to go through the thousands of letters that Kennedy received from kids every week. Through a friend of mine who was an attorney for NBC in Washington, my request was put through to Pierre Salinger.

Salinger raised no objection but he did comment when the request was made that he couldn't understand why anyone would want to go through all the mail from kids. I, of course, knew that a good book could be structured from those letters.

I quickly sold the book to Larry Hughes at William Morrow who shared my enthusiasm for the project, and the necessary arrangements were made. I was instructed to present myself at one of the White House gates and ask for the man in charge of the mailroom. The guard at the gate directly in front of the White House was pleasant enough and checked my name on his visitors' roster.

"Do you have any identification?" the guard asked me. I hadn't been prepared for that question, and I suddenly realized that the only identification I had with me was my Diners Club card. Somehow that didn't seem appropriate so I thought again and remembered that I also had a laminated photostat of my army discharge.

I handed the guard the photostat; he glanced at it and picked up the phone. "There's a Corporal Adler who has an appointment at the mailroom." I guess to the guard at the White House once in the military always in the military.

The White House mailroom was located in the basement of the Executive Office Building on the White House grounds across a small driveway directly opposite the White House itself. The people in the mailroom couldn't have been nicer as they showed me to a desk they had set aside for me in a room where all the mail sent to the president from kids was sorted by state.

It was half-past nine in the morning when I started to go through the mail. Since I couldn't take the actual letters with me I had to copy in longhand those I wanted to include in the book. Once I began to work on the letters I knew that the material was going to be even better than I had hoped.

I kept copying those kids' letters to Kennedy without stop all morning and through lunch and on into the afternoon. At five o'clock the mailroom employees began to leave. By five-thirty I was virtually alone when the man in charge of the mailroom came over to tell me it was time to call it a day.

I was dismayed because, although I had copied a lot of letters, I still needed more, and I didn't know when I could get permission to return to the White House mailroom.

The gentleman in charge must have noticed the consternation on my face because he quickly said, "You don't have to leave if you aren't finished yet. Just make sure you turn out the lights when you leave."

I thanked him profusely as he left and I continued, alone, in the White House mailroom to copy those marvelous letters. At about half-past nine a guard came by and nodded but didn't ask any questions. He just assumed I belonged there.

An hour later with my hand about to fall off, I decided it was time to leave since by then I had copied all the letters I needed for the book. I turned out the lights and left the mailroom. It was an eerie feeling to walk outside the Executive Office Building late in the evening all alone and only a few feet across from the White House itself.

Nobody bothered me or came rushing toward me to ask what I was doing all alone at that hour on the grounds of the White House. I strolled briskly toward the gate which at that hour seemed like an interminable walk. I was certain that at any second, six Secret Service men would surround me or perhaps, I fantasized, John F. Kennedy would yell from the White House and ask what I was doing there.

What was most puzzling was the fact that I was certain that no one in Pierre Salinger's office had really checked me out when the request had been made. "What do they know about me?" I muttered to myself. "Asking to go through the letters could have been a ruse to get on the White House grounds."

Maybe it was my honest face. Or perhaps it was because the guard at the White House gate knew that I had served my country during the Korean War and that I had been honorably discharged as a corporal—not exactly a command rank.

As I finally reached the gate I grew even more apprehensive that I would be stopped and questioned and, who knows, even arrested for strolling on the White House grounds after dark.

Nothing even close to that happened.

When I approached the gate, the guard on duty put down the newspaper he was reading and waved as I walked past his sentry post.

Finally, I was on Pennsylvania Avenue and as I glanced at the White House over my shoulder I kept hoping that someday soon the White House would improve their security. I even thought of writing a letter to the White House mailroom to that effect but I didn't.

Kids' Letters to President Kennedy was a success and my solitary moment on the White House grounds has up to now been a story I have told only to my closest friends.

Despite the fact that I have been in book publishing for more than twenty years, I continue to be amazed at the things that happen.

For a number of years I represented an author of nonfiction books who had been moderately successful and certainly had been a cut above the run-of-the-mill author. The author's third book was to be an autobiography—which I encouraged the author to write. There was no question that I was the catalyst for the autobiography.

Unfortunately, the idea was turned down by more than twenty publishers but I continued to believe that the book was salable.

One day out of the blue, I received a phone call from the author saying that he had decided to give the book to another agent to represent. Since I didn't have a contract with the author there was little I could do about the matter.

Three months later I learned through publishing sources that the book had been sold to a major book publisher. What makes the story most unusual was the fact that the publisher who bought the book was one of the publishers I had submitted the book to originally. There had been a change of guard and management at the publishing firm and the new people in charge decided they wanted the book.

The point of the story is, of course, that even if a firm turns you down once, you can go back to the other people at the house—assuming, of course, that management has changed or that the book was never presented to the top decision makers in the first place.

I knew the first time I saw him on "60 Minutes" that Andy Rooney was a book property. He has everything going for him. He is on one of the most popular television programs ("60 Minutes" has always been in the top ten over the last four years) but most important of all, "60 Minutes" has an audience that is more likely to buy books than, say, the audience for "Dallas." Andy Rooney is witty and often wise and his commentaries at the close of each week's edition of "60 Minutes" are highly entertaining.

I aggressively pursued Andy Rooney for a book but as things turned out I pursued him perhaps a little too aggressively.

More than two years ago I arranged a phone introduction to Andy Rooney through a friend who had been a producer for "60 Minutes." I guess I could have asked Rather or Wallace to introduce me to Rooney but I preferred not to.

My initial phone conversation with Andy Rooney went something like this:

Adler: Andy, could we get together for lunch perhaps?

Rooney: I'm not sure I want to write a book and if I did I don't know why I would need an agent.

Adler: I can understand that but why don't we have lunch at the Four Seasons anyway and perhaps I can answer any questions you might have about book publishing.

Rooney: Well, I guess there's no harm in that.

Andy Rooney and I met for lunch the next week at the Four Seasons. I immediately liked him. He had an honest, down-to-earth quality and he was easy to talk to. For most of the lunch our conversation wandered from subject to subject until finally we got around to books. It was clear to me that despite his previous protests, Andy Rooney was seriously thinking about writing a book and I thought as we came close to ordering our coffee that perhaps he would become an author after all and that I would represent him.

I have learned over the years that most celebrities are reluctant debutantes when it comes to writing a book. I have frequently heard such comments as: "Who would read my book?" "I don't think I have anything to say." "Maybe I'll write something when I retire."

In Andy Rooney's case, two things were clear. The first was that he could write—he writes his own commentaries for "60 Minutes"—and secondly, he recognized that his exposure on television presented a unique opportunity.

After I presented what I thought was a strong case in favor of his writing a book now, Rooney said he would think about it. As we left the Four Seasons I thought I had a fifty-fifty chance of representing the resident wit on television's most popular news magazine.

But then I blew it.

I forgot the advice I have often given to myself. When you think you have made the sale or are close to making the sale, know when to say "good-bye." Don't overstay your welcome because if you do you are liable to say something that will cause the other party to change his or her mind or reconsider.

As we were leaving the Four Seasons, I asked Andy where he was heading and he said to the bank. I volunteered to walk him to the bank since it was in the general direction of my office. As we were getting close to the bank, I commented that there was another reason he should write a book.

"What's that?" Rooney asked.

"The money," I remarked. "The money you could make on a book could be considerable."

"I'm really not interested in doing a book for the money," Andy replied.

I should have stopped right there but I continued to press the issue. "Well, Andy," I said, "the money you can make on a book can give you more independence."

Andy made no further comment and departed cordially.

The next day I sent Andy Rooney a brief letter by messenger telling him how much I had enjoyed our lunch and repeating that I thought there would be a wide audience for his book and that I would like to represent him.

A short time later I received a note from Andy that he had obviously typed himself. In effect, Rooney kissed me off as a possible agent for any book he might write.

"You're really only interested in the money," Andy told me in his brief note, and as I read those words I knew there would be no way of convincing Rooney that money was not my only motivation.

Andy Rooney, of course, finally did write his book titled *A Few Minutes with Andy Rooney* which was published by Atheneum. To date, Rooney's book has sold over 100,000 copies and as of the writing of this book is number three on the *New York Times* Best Sellers list.

I wish him well. I never doubted for a second that Andy Rooney was a bestseller.

Today it is fashionable for well-known personalities to write novels drawing heavily upon their personal experiences. F. Lee Bailey, Marvin Kalb, Margaret Truman and Jack Anderson all have written novels, and in most cases they have done well.

The very first of these was a novel I developed with Scott Meredith. At the time, Meredith was my agent and Bill Adler Books had developed several books with him for some of his authors.

Scott is very creative and imaginative at developing book packages. One day, I suggested to Scott that there would be good potential if we could publish a novel called *The Senator* written by somebody who had an insider's view of the Senate. Scott agreed that it was a good idea and immediately thought of Drew Pearson as the best possible author.

At the time, Drew Pearson was the best-known Washington columnist in the country and he had been at it for a long, long time.

Pearson knew more about the Senate and senators than practically anyone but, more important, he was a national personality and *The Senator* by Drew Pearson would attract wide attention. Pearson was definitely a brand name.

The Senator by Drew Pearson was a big hit. It made money for everybody and paved the way for a whole new genre of books—the "brand name" novel.

Halfway through the Iranian hostage crisis, I received a phone call from Joel Sorkin who had been recommended to me by another agent, something that occasionally happens when an agent can't handle a certain book because of a conflict with another book or because it isn't the kind of book that the agent feels comfortable with.

Joel Sorkin, as it turned out, was the cousin of Barry Rosen, one of the hostages. Sorkin came to see me and told me that Rosen's wife, Barbara, was interested in exploring the possibility of Barry's writing a book when he was released.

I was, of course, more than mildly interested and told Sorkin I would like to meet with Mrs. Rosen. It was arranged and I sent a limousine to Barbara's apartment in Brooklyn where she was living with Barry's parents and her two small children.

Barbara Rosen is an attractive young woman who was a little apprehensive at our first meeting. She appeared uncomfortable discussing a book by her husband while he was still a prisoner in Iran, but yet she wanted to explore all the possibilities.

I explained everything I could, including all of the financial aspects. Barbara kept repeating that she couldn't make a commitment for Barry while he was still a prisoner but if Barry wanted to do a book she felt it was important to be ready to move ahead quickly.

I agreed to the extent that I was certain that some of the other hostages would probably also want to write books when they were released. I suggested to Barbara that if and when the book was written, it should be by *both* of them since the ordeal had been not only difficult for Barry but for Barbara as well. "In a sense, Barbara," I told her, "you have both been prisoners of the Iranians."

Shortly after my first meeting with Barbara Rosen, and while Barry and the other hostages still faced an uncertain fate, I arranged for Barbara to meet with Sherry Arden at William Morrow and Harvey Ginsberg, one of the senior editors. We again covered the possibilities of a book by the Rosens, and Barbara, although she was noncommittal, was certainly very interested in the possibility of a book.

I assured Barbara that I would keep our meeting and conversations confidential until Barry was released. Barbara and I agreed that a story about her meeting with a book publisher while her husband was still in Iranian hands might not be understood if it appeared in the papers.

I kept in touch with Barbara by mail and phone and then the glorious day arrived when the hostages were finally given their freedom. Less than twelve hours after they were released, I was the most surprised man in New York when I read an item in the *New York Post* to the effect that Morton Janklow would be representing Barbara and Barry Rosen.

My initial reaction was to pick up the phone and blast Joel Sorkin, who had not only asked me to represent Barbara but a book project of his own. I decided not to make the call.

The hostages returned triumphantly to New York, and less than a week later I received a phone call from Barbara Rosen asking if she and Barry could come in to see me. "Of course," I told her. I surmised that the *Post* story must have been wrong.

I liked Barry Rosen. He was bright, considerate and clearly tired and a little bewildered by all that had happened. We chatted for about an hour and toward the end of our conversation, Barbara Rosen told me that I was the first of four agents they would be meeting with during the next few days. I asked who the other agents were and she told me. (Janklow was one of them.)

All of the agents were first-rate and I assured Barry and Barbara that whomever they selected they would be in good hands. They chose Julian Bach who sold the Rosens' story to Doubleday, and the book will soon be published.

I guess the first is not always the winner.

Alexander Haig is one of the very best book properties who has yet to write his book and I jumped at the chance to meet him. At the time, General Haig was commander-in-chief of NATO but he had just announced that he was retiring, and there was strong speculation that Haig would seek the Republican presidential nomination in 1980.

Through Harry Walker, the well-known New York lecture agent, I was given an introduction to Haig, and it was suggested that I write to the general at his NATO headquarters in Europe. My one-page letter asked Haig if I could meet with him when I was in Europe on my next business trip—about a month away.

I received a quick reply from one of Haig's assistants telling me that the general would be in Paris at the Ritz Hotel on a certain date and that I could meet with him then.

No sooner had Gloria and I checked into our room at the Ritz when the phone rang. It was an aide of General Haig's confirming my appointment for the following day at two o'clock. As it happened, Haig was staying in a suite on the same floor as our room.

Promptly at two I presented myself at Haig's spacious three-room suite and was greeted by a military aide who quickly disappeared to leave Haig and me alone over coffee. My first impression of Alexander Haig was that he was very handsome and that he chain smoked and drank a lot of black coffee. My second impression was that he asked questions—all kinds of questions.

Haig immediately told me that he was going to explore a number of options when he left NATO and that one of them might be to run for public office in Pennsylvania. He also said that he was going to lecture and that he had received many offers from large corporations to serve on their boards of directors or in an executive capacity.

I made my pitch for Haig to consider a book as one of his options, and it was then that the questions began in earnest. The general wanted to know everything from the size of the advance he could expect from a publisher (I told him at least a quarter of a million dollars, if not more) to how long it would take to have a book published. He wanted to know everything about how book publishing worked. I don't ever recall meeting with anyone who asked so many penetrating questions.

As I answered each of the general's questions he made notes on a yellow legal pad, smoking and drinking coffee as he wrote.

Finally, after an hour, I had told Haig all there was to know about the book business, and I had the feeling that he was now the best informed general in the world about publishing. Not once did Haig commit himself to a book but his interest was obviously there.

As our conversation came to a close—it was more of an interview than a conversation, with Haig doing the interviewing—the general thanked me for my time and said if he wanted to pursue the matter he would be in touch with me. I left with Haig lighting up yet another cigarette and I returned to our room down the hall.

Gloria was waiting for me when I returned. "How did it go?" she asked.

"Well," I replied, "Alexander Haig knows enough now about book publishing to be his own agent if he decides to write a book."

"Will he?"

"Someday," I told Gloria, "but not now. I sensed that he has other things on his mind."

"Then why all his questions?"

"He likes to have options. Besides, now that he knows all the answers, he'll probably ask Swifty Lazar to make a million-dollar deal for him. I only promised $250,000."

Alexander Haig has yet to write his book, but someday he will, and when he does he certainly will not be an author without all the facts.

You can never tell where a book project is going to come from.

I have always had a crush on Jane Pauley and was anxious to put together a book for her. My friend Ralph Mann, who is the chairman of ICM and Jane's agent, arranged for the three of us to have lunch to discuss the possibility of a book.

Jane was, as I expected she would be, lovely, bright and easy to talk to, with a delightful and warm personality. We discussed all kinds of book projects but Jane didn't seem very interested.

The luncheon almost ended on a catastrophic note. I went to the men's room just before we finished and the zipper on my trousers broke. I was a little uncomfortable pulling down my jacket to cover the broken zipper during the few minutes we had to wait for the check, but fortunately I made it out of the restaurant without Jane or Ralph noticing.

Jane never did go ahead with a book, and it was almost a year later when Tom Brokaw called to ask if I would appear on the "Today" show to discuss the possibilities for books to be written by the former Iranian hostages.

"By the way," Tom told me, "Jane will be conducting the

interview." Nothing could have pleased me more. I still had a crush on Jane (even more so after my lunch with her), and I welcomed the opportunity to talk to her again. (Never say die, Adler.)

The next day Brokaw called again to confirm my date the following day and to go over the areas we would be discussing on the program. "Incidentally," Brokaw said at the close of our phone call, "Jane won't be on the program tomorrow so Jessica Savitch will interview you."

My heart sank. It wasn't that I had anything against Jessica but it was just that I had been looking forward to my interview with Jane.

The next morning I arrived at the NBC studios bright and early, and as we were standing off camera waiting to go on, I casually mentioned to Jessica that she should consider writing a book. Jessica nodded that she might be interested.

I moved quickly because I instinctively felt that Jessica Savitch could be a major book property. The reasons were clear to me. First of all, Jessica was one of the best journalists in broadcasting, and year after year she had always been voted one of the best-known and respected women in the country. Most importantly, Jessica was one of the first anchorwomen on network television.

The next morning Jessica and I met for coffee at NBC and she agreed to write the book. I didn't waste any time. The first publisher I approached was interested but wanted to meet Jessica first. I thought that was an unnecessary step and I immediately called Phyllis Grann, the editor-in-chief at Putnam's, and one hour later we had made a sizable deal.

Jessica was delighted. The entire time from our first meeting on the "Today" show to a book contract was less than a week.

I am still fond of Jane Pauley but Jessica Savitch has become one of my favorite clients. She is bright, attractive and motivated, and her book when published (it's almost finished) will be a major bestseller.

Over the years I have had all sorts of book deals brought to me to represent. There have been at least four former CIA agents who have wanted to write the "truth" about the CIA and more than a dozen convicted criminals, including two murderers, who have wanted to tell their sordid stories.

Only a year ago, I received a phone call from the attorney of a man who was on trial in a celebrated murder case. The attorney said that his client was ready to spill the beans about his life of crime in return for

$200,000. I rejected the attorney's offer as I have in the cases of all men or women convicted of violent crimes.

Today, however, many enterprising attorneys obtain the book rights from their clients as part of their fees, and in some instances the attorneys have been able to sell the book or movie rights for a considerable sum of money. Who says that crime doesn't pay!

Perhaps the most unusual book project involved an attractive young woman who wanted to become a call girl, keep a diary and then write a book about her experiences as a high-priced hooker. She was fresh out of college and certainly not the type you would expect to want to write such a book.

"Why do you want to do it?" I asked her when she first met with me.

"Well," she replied, "I've never been a call girl or anything like that and I could write an honest book about what it is like—what the call girls are like and what the men are like."

My initial reaction was to walk away from the project and, although I had to admit it was an intriguing idea, I wasn't even sure I could find a publisher for such an unlikely book.

There was another factor. I was certain that the book would receive more than negative comment from feminists although that didn't overly concern me.

I decided to go ahead with the book, and much to my surprise I quickly secured a publisher. The advance was $10,000 and the young woman eagerly proceeded with the book.

Somehow she got to know a few call girls who agreed to find some "customers" for her. She never revealed to the other girls that she was writing a book, and as far as they were concerned, she was just another woman who had decided to make some money at the world's oldest profession.

Periodically, my client would phone me with a progress report. "I saw a nice 'john' from Chicago," she would say, "and I made $100. I'm keeping a careful record of everything they say. You wouldn't believe some of the remarks these 'johns' make."

After six months, the phone calls stopped coming and when I tried to call her I found her phone had been disconnected.

She disappeared and so did the book project.

The birth of a book and its eventual publication can often have an unusual beginning.

I was once representing a rather well-known author who had written a number of bestselling books but at the time he was looking for a book project. He came to see me in the hope that I could develop a commercial book for him.

I suggested a book titled *All in the First Family: The Presidents' Kinfolk* which would be about all our presidents' relatives from George Washington to Ronald Reagan.

The writer loved the idea and asked me to go ahead and see if I could find a publisher. I did just that. Putnam's liked the project and offered an advance of $30,000. The writer was satisfied with the advance although he wasn't thrilled.

When I sent the contract to the author, he wasn't at all happy because the publisher was going to pay only $5,000 when the contract was signed and the remainder of the advance as the book progressed. Since the writer hadn't written one word of the book—not even an outline—I didn't think the contract offered was unfair.

"I'm not going to do it," the writer told me and so we parted.

I still thought *All in the First Family* was a good idea and I decided to make a counterproposal to Ellis Amburn, the editor at Putnam's. I told him I would do the book for them myself for $20,000. Since I was a successfully published author I didn't feel at all reluctant in making that counterproposal.

I was positive that Putnam's would not pay me $30,000 to write the book, but they might pay $20,000.

Ellis said he would get back to me, and a few days later he called to say that the book was mine for $20,000.

Instead of a commission of $4,500 which I would have made on the advance of $30,000, I now had another book of my own for which I would make considerably more.

I recently sold a self-help book to a medium-sized New York publisher. The advance was a modest $15,000 but, because of the subject of the book, the publisher had high hopes that we might have a bestseller. "I think this could be a winner—really big," the publisher kept telling me shortly after we signed the contract.

This publisher, not unlike some other publishers, liked to sell paperback rights before the book was published. He believed that it was safer to sell paperback rights before publication because if the book bombed he might never be able to sell the paperback rights. In this particular case

I went along with the publisher, especially because he seemed so confident of making, as he put it, "at least a six-figure advance." Since the initial advance was only $15,000, a $100,000 paperback sale would appear to be a very good reprint sale.

The publisher started to submit the finished manuscript to the major paperback publishers and the early signs were very good. "We have a lot of interest," he told me joyfully over the phone. "It may even go to middle six figures."

As the weeks went by, one by one the paperback publishers began to grow lukewarm to the book. "I still have two who are very interested," the publisher said, "and I think we are going to make it."

At the same time, the publisher decided to sell the first serial rights to one of the women's magazines and he was as confident of a major magazine sale as he was of a paperback sale. Again, the early interest was strong and the publisher, along with his director of subsidiary rights, decided to auction off the magazine rights.

The auction was held and it was like having a party with no guests. There were no bids. None at all. Although disappointed, the publisher was determined to press on with the two remaining paperback houses that still seemed interested.

"I had hoped," the publisher told me, "that if we had made a first serial sale, it would have helped us with the paperback people." The publisher's comment was symptomatic of book publishing. One sale feeds on another.

The publisher started to work on the two remaining paperback publishers but the book was rejected in short order, and he was left with no paperback offers. "I think we have a real problem," the publisher told me a short time later over the phone. "Unless something happens the book is dead."

"Dead!" I thought to myself as I hung up the phone. "The book hasn't even been published yet and won't be for another three months."

I've decided to keep the publisher in this particular story anonymous because I don't want to affect his future dealings with authors or agents, but I did think his attitude was ludicrous although, I must admit, it is not so unusual in book publishing today.

More than anything else, book publishing has become a business of selling rights—first serial, book club, paperback, foreign, motion picture and eventually, video cassette, rights. The most important person at any publishing house is likely to be the director of subsidiary rights.

More often than not, books are dead before they are published, and the actual process of publishing and distributing the book to stores is an exercise in futility.

"How many quotes can we get for the book?" an editor asked me recently a few weeks before the book was to be presented at a sales conference. "We really need some pre-pub quotes," the editor insisted, "otherwise, I don't think we will be able to excite the sales force or the bookstores."

"I'll see what I can do," I told the editor, since the book in question was one I had written.

The quote business is big in book publishing. Almost daily, manuscripts, uncorrected galleys or bound books are sent by authors and editors to people whose quote might add to the sales potential of a book. A good quote ("great book" or "marvelous read" or a "landmark book") is supposed to help the sale of a book—not just to the public but to the publisher's sales organization and to the bookstores as well.

Obviously, the quote has to come from some authority or celebrity or another well-known author. For a nonfiction book, a quote from William Safire or Edwin Newman or William Buckley is like four stars for a restaurant since they are so literate and articulate themselves.

Quotes and introductions have been obsessions with publishers and, like so many things today in book publishing, the quote business is highly overrated and not so effective as many publishers believe it is.

Dan Rather recently gave a marvelous quote for a first-rate book that I represented, but as far as I can determine the Rather quote, plus some other good quotes the author had received, had little or no effect on the sale of the book.

Quotes can help but they are not a panacea and I doubt if many books have become bestsellers because of their quotes or introductions.

Perhaps the best summary of the quote business is revealed in a letter I recently received from Art Buchwald when I asked him for a quote for one of my books, *Kids' Letters to President Reagan:* "Thanks so much for your note—the problem is I don't do blurbs. I went out of the blurb business about seven years ago at a time when all my friends were writing books—some good, some bad. They all wanted me to write something for them and life became impossible. I took a vow never to write a blurb again, and I have stuck to it. Believe me, it makes life much less complicated."

Ralph Nader is a remarkable man—a pleasant, decent, bright individual—but as a client for a literary agent, Nader can be tough.

A number of years ago, I sold a book for Nader to Simon & Schuster. (The book was never published because Nader subsequently abandoned the project.)

I had no trouble getting an advance that was satisfactory to Nader for his book, but the problems began when Nader began to put his pencil to many of the clauses he objected to in the Simon & Schuster contract. I was able to get most of the changes in the contract that Nader wanted but the one thing that Simon & Schuster would not change to Nader's satisfaction had to do with the liability clause in case of a lawsuit against Nader or S & S for libel, plagiarism or some other reason.

The liability clause in most publishers' contracts requires the author to indemnify the publisher in case there is a suit against the author or publisher and they should lose. In such a case, if the author is at fault, he or she has to pay all the publishers' damages.

Nader refused to indemnify S & S beyond a maximum limit of $25,000. "I've never been sued," Nader told me and John Diamond, the capable vice president and general counsel at S & S who has since gone into a successful private practice.

But S & S wouldn't budge because the liability clause is one of the most important in any publishing contract as far as the publisher is concerned. It protects the publisher in case the author says something in his or her book that is libelous or plagiarizes someone else.

Nader was against the liability clause on principle and it was clear that unless Nader or S & S softened his position the deal was going to fall through. I didn't want that to happen and I offered a suggestion to both S & S and Nader that I hoped could resolve the situation. It was, to say the least, an unusual solution but it did resolve the matter.

Bill Adler Books, Inc. agreed to take on the responsibility for the author's liability and such a clause was actually written into the contract. If Nader had written the book and there had been a suit that was lost by S & S and Nader, we would, of course, have lost much more than a commission, but I thought it was a risk-free gesture. Anything for a sale.

Perhaps two of the most unusual sales I have ever made as an author, agent or book packager were to Bernard Geis who in many ways has been one of the more creative publishers over the last twenty years. Today Bernard Geis is primarily a book packager.

It was Geis who first published Jacqueline Susann as a novelist and, of course, her first novel, *Valley of the Dolls*, started her on her phenomenal career as one of the most popular novelists of our time.

The two sales I made to Geis were for ideas for two novels. Only the ideas were sold to Geis and it was agreed that I would search for writers to execute each of the novels. It was probably the first time that a publisher had paid for two novel ideas yet to be written.

Although the payments from Geis were not overwhelming, they did "lock up" the ideas for Geis while I looked for the writers. To date, the ideas are still just ideas.

Perhaps the most unusual book deal that I ever represented involved two well-known Hollywood personalities.

I was sitting in my office one day when I received a phone call from a Hollywood personality with a national reputation. "Mr. A and I would like to write a book," he told me.

"Great," I replied, "I'll be in California next week and we can have dinner and discuss it." Of course, Mr. A was identified to me over the phone but I promised not to reveal his identity or the identity of the person who called me whom I shall refer to as Mr. B.

I had dinner with A and B at an out-of-the-way Hollywood restaurant and we discussed the book they wanted to write. I was very excited about representing A and B because I was confident that the book they had in mind could be a major bestseller.

A and B wanted to keep their identities confidential, not for any sinister or illegal reason, but because they believed (and rightly so) that there was no need to reveal that they were writing a book until the book was finished and ready to be published.

There were two good reasons for that. First, because they were national figures the speculation about their book could interfere with their work and second, there was always the possibility that for one reason or another the book might not be finished and published, so there was no need to cause speculation and discussion about a book that might not be published.

As we discussed the book at dinner at that Hollywood restaurant, I was hopeful that I could find a publisher who would be willing to sign a contract for a book with our company for the two authors whose identity would have to be secret.

The next morning I called the president of a major publishing firm. The conversation went something like this:

Adler: I have a book for you that could be a major bestseller.

Publisher: What is it about?

Adler: I can't tell you.

Publisher: Who is the author?

Adler: There are two authors. They are prominent Hollywood figures. I can't reveal who the authors are right now. You'll have to sign a contract with our company for a book by authors A and B.

Publisher: How much is this mysterious book going to cost me?

I told the publisher the size of the advance—and it was a healthy amount. I waited a few seconds while the publisher mulled over the proposal.

"Okay," responded the publisher, "I trust your judgment. I'll take the chance."

The contract was signed and the book by A and B is now being written and is close to completion. Although the ending to this story has yet to be told, I am confident it is going to end positively with a bestseller.

At the very least, it was certainly an unusual deal in a business where deals become more unusual every day.

I consider it the "perfect" book package and it started with a chance meeting at a party with Bess Myerson.

Bess Myerson is, of course, a former Miss America, a one-time candidate for the U.S. Senate from New York, the former commissioner of consumer affairs for the City of New York, and a well-known television personality, author, lecturer and newspaper columnist.

Bess and I had known each other on and off over the years but we hadn't seen each other for a few years. When we met, Bess and I remarked to each other that we looked thinner than the last time we had met.

After a few minutes of conversation, Bess and I determined that we had both lost weight and maintained our weight loss as a result of following the diet published in pamphlet form by the Bureau of Nutrition of the Department of Health of the City of New York.

"Bess," I said, "you and I should do a book based on that diet. After all, it has worked for both of us."

"You're right," Bess Myerson replied. "It would be wonderful to have a diet book published that not only can help you lose weight but won't hurt you like some of the fad diets can."

I determined then and there that Bess and I were going to do a diet book, but the big question in my mind was how was I going to package the book in order to create some excitement and attention. What the industry didn't need was yet another diet book that nobody would buy. There were plenty of that kind of diet book already.

A few days later the idea came to me. Since the diet that had worked for both Bess and me was a diet developed by the city, why not call it *The I Love New York Diet*? I especially liked that title because the words and design for "I Love New York" with its special lettering and heart were known and recognizable not only in all fifty states but around the world.

Millions of dollars had been spent promoting the "I Love New York" logo and it was a highly visible and promotable brand name. "I Love New York" has appeared on everything from T-shirts to ashtrays—so why not a diet book, especially this diet book.

The next day I met with Sherry Arden of William Morrow and Al Marchioni, the executive vice president. In less than five minutes, Sherry and Al agreed to publish *The I Love New York Diet* by Bess Myerson and Bill Adler.

Bess and I, along with the assistance of a superb medical researcher and writer, Harold Prince, began to work on expanding the brief diet developed by the city's Bureau of Nutrition into a full-length diet book of 40,000 words. We wanted to complete the manuscript quickly so that the book could be published in January, one of the best months to publish a weight loss book. January is a good time because most people overeat during the Christmas and New Year holidays. (Just before summer is another good time for diet books when people are beginning to worry about how they will look in a bathing suit.)

Since we had conceived the idea for the book in July, we didn't have very much time if it was to be published in January. William Morrow had actually given us forty-five days to complete the manuscript and if it weren't for the unique talents of Harold Prince, we would never had made it.

The next problem or creative challenge that we faced was that Bess Myerson and I knew it would be helpful for the sale of the book if we could get some recommendations for the diet from some well-known physicians.

It is difficult to get doctors to recommend a diet book because most diet books are not medically sound, but I knew that we had a diet that was developed and tested by the Bureau of Nutrition and that would be acceptable to most physicians.

As soon as the manuscript was finished, I sent a copy to Dr. Myron Winick, the director of the prestigious Institute of Human Nutrition at Columbia University and asked him if he would write an introduction to *The I Love New York Diet*. He liked the book and thought it was a helpful and worthwhile diet and agreed to write a three-page introduction. Dr. Winick has a reputation as one of the country's leading nutritionists and I knew his introduction would mean a lot to the success of the book.

In addition to Dr. Winick's introduction, we were fortunate in receiving recommendations from several top doctors, including Dr. Herbert Benson, Associate Professor of Medicine at Harvard Medical School and director of the Division of Behavioral Medicine at Boston's Beth Israel Hospital; Dr. Henry Heimlich, originator of the livesaving Heimlich maneuver; Dr. Richard Winter, chairman of the board of the Executive Health Group; Dr. Daniel Foster, Professor of Internal Medicine, University of Texas Health Science Center in Dallas and Dr. Nicholas Pace, Assistant Professor of Clinical Medicine at New York University's School of Medicine.

These doctors agreed to let us use their names and recommendations in advertising and promotion and on the jacket of the book. Their comments made a big difference in the ultimate success of *The I Love New York Diet*.

Although, as I mentioned earlier in this chapter, I believe the "quote game" in book publishing is overdone, I felt that some celebrity quotes would put the icing on our cake. I quickly obtained quotable quotes from Howard Cosell, Dick Clark, Ron Nessen, Lyn Revson, Suzy Chaffee, Larry King, Art Linkletter and Joan Lunden—all endorsing the principles of *The I Love New York Diet*.

The celebrity quotes and the recommendations from the doctors were all received in time to be put on the endpapers of the book and the Morrow art and production department did a brilliant job on the jacket design, capturing the "I Love New York" logo.

The first printing for *The I Love New York Diet* was 50,000 copies, and the book was selected by the Literary Guild and *Woman's Day* magazine, which paid for second serial rights a price equal to the advance payment we received.

It is fair to say that *before* it was published *The I Love New York Diet* was a hit and as of the writing of this book, it is number six on the *New York Times* Best Sellers list with more than 100,000 copies in print.

On more than one occasion, I have lost major book properties because I was either too early or too late.

Take the case of the Sophia Loren beauty book.

A while ago, I had a meeting with an advertising and promotion man who was well connected in the cosmetics industry and during the course of our conversation Sophia Loren's name came up because of the new line of Sophia Loren perfume.

"I'd like to get to Sophia and see if she would be interested in writing a beauty book," I told my friend.

"No problem," he replied. "I'll put you in touch with the president of the company that is making the Sophia Loren perfume. I'm sure they will be interested. It's a fine idea."

True to his word, my friend did just that, and the next day I was on the phone with the cosmetics company making a pitch for the Sophia Loren beauty book. I received a very positive reaction and was told they would get back to me but they never did, and I never pursued the matter any further, assuming that the idea was dead.

I forgot about the Sophia Loren beauty book. Almost nine months later, I was having lunch with Jonathan Dolger, an agent who had been a senior editor at Simon & Schuster and at Harper & Row.

"What's exciting?" I asked him.

"Well," Jonathan replied, "we just finished the contracts for a big book for William Morrow and Ballantine."

"What book?"

"The Sophia Loren beauty book," Jonathan told me.

I never did bother to ask Jonathan how he got to represent the book, but it was obvious that I had either been too early or too late or that I had just plain dropped the ball.

June Allyson, Connie Francis, Diahann Carroll, Eddie Fisher and Gary Crosby were all celebrities I had approached (or whose agents I'd approached) about books, and in each instance I was either too early—they weren't ready to write their stories—or I was too late—they already had contracts. Timing is *everything* in getting a book property and so is persistence, as I learned from the Sophia Loren beauty book.

All the celebrities I have just mentioned now have book contracts with other agents and are either writing their stories or have already had their books published.

Sometimes a chance meeting can result in a major book contract.

About six months ago, my wife and I were invited by a friend to attend the annual Friars Club dinner. I wasn't that anxious to go because I would have to rent a tuxedo (It was a black tie dinner and I don't own a tuxedo) and because Friars Club dinners usually have at least ten comedians performing. After the first three it can get a little repetitive. How many dirty jokes can you listen to in one evening?

But the guest of honor was going to be Burt Reynolds, and Johnny Carson was the toastmaster so we decided to go.

It turned out to be a very wise decision.

Sitting next to us at the dinner was Irving Mansfield who not only has had a remarkable career as a television producer but was for more than thirty years Jacqueline Susann's husband and partner in her extraordinary career.

Jackie, of course, died of cancer a number of years ago, and her death ended a career that had led to more number one bestsellers than any other fiction writer with the possible exception of James Michener.

Irving is a charming man and a brilliant raconteur. During the course of the evening I casually asked Irving why he hadn't written a book about his life and his life with Jackie.

It was obvious from Irving's reply that he had thought about the idea but for personal reasons he was not prepared to write such a book.

Irving, Gloria and I enjoyed one another's company at the Friars Club dinner and we met a few weeks later for a quiet dinner together. As it happens so often in book publishing, one thing led to another and by the next time we met for dinner, Irving and I were talking seriously about his book.

I am sure that one of the factors that motivated Irving to consider a book was our developing relationship and, I like to think, his confidence in me and my ability to shepherd the book to its successful publication.

Two months later, Irving Mansfield and I were in the office of Louis Wolfe, the president and chief executive officer of Bantam Books. We made the deal at that meeting for Bantam to publish the hardcover and paperback editions of Irving Mansfield's book about his own life and his life with Jackie.

It was a major book deal for very serious money and as I write this,

Irving, working with journalist Jean Libman Block, is completing his manuscript on a book that is destined to be a bestseller not only in the United States but around the world.

It was a lucky break that I went to that Friars Club dinner because not only did I secure a superb book property but the friendship of a wonderful human being.

Frank Sinatra recently recorded a song titled "To Love a Child" with lyrics by Hal David and music by Joe Raposo. That song started as a book that will soon be published.

Here's what happened.

After Nancy Reagan became First Lady, she increased her efforts on behalf of the Foster Grandparents program, a nonprofit organization she had first become interested in when she was First Lady of California. Mrs. Reagan had even filmed some public service commercials for the Foster Grandparents program after moving to the White House.

It was while watching one of Mrs. Reagan's public service commercials that I got the idea for the book based on some of the more dramatic stories of foster grandparents and the children with whom they have become involved and helped. A few days after the idea occurred to me, I was on the phone with Nancy Reagan proposing a book titled *To Love a Child.*

Mrs. Reagan was interested, especially when I assured her that I could secure a major publisher (we quickly did—Bobbs-Merrill) and that all advances and royalties would go to the Foster Grandparents program.

After some discussions at the White House, I was given the green light and the book contract was prepared.

Less than a week later, Gloria and I were having dinner with Anne and Hal David. Anne David is an author and a client and Hal David is one of the most successful lyricists of our time and the current president of ASCAP.

As we were finishing our dinner at the Four Seasons, I casually asked Hal if he could write a song about the Foster Grandparents idea titled "To Love a Child." Hal, a talented and affable man, loved the title and the idea. Less than one month later Hal, collaborating with the equally talented Joe Raposo, had completed the song.

The song was sung and played by Joe Raposo for Mrs. Reagan at the ASCAP headquarters on one of the First Lady's visits to New York. Mrs. Reagan loved the song and her first choice was for Sinatra to record it.

Everyone concerned is hopeful that the song and the book will enrich the Foster Grandparents program and assist them in their fine work.

I was pleased to have been the catalyst for the book and the song.

Simon & Schuster once published a book that was the result of an author's party given by another publisher.

I had been invited to a book party in Washington by another publisher and at the party was Lorne Greene, the television and motion picture star who is best known for his role in the long running television series, "Bonanza."

I had a few casual words with Lorne Greene at the party and followed up our meeting a few days later with a phone call and a book idea.

Lorne Greene had long been associated with animals as a result of a television series he had hosted and his commercials for Alpo dog food. I suggested to Lorne that he write a book called *God's Remarkable Creatures*—a book of unusual and dramatic animal stories. Lorne liked the idea and gave me the go-ahead to find a publisher.

The first publisher I talked to, Simon & Schuster, bought the book and with Peter Schwed as the editor, the book was successfully published a few years ago.

The point of the story is, of course, that books can come from anywhere—even another publisher's cocktail party.

14

Celebrities Who Have Known Me

BILL Adler Books has probably represented more celebrities than any other literary agency with the possible exception of Swifty Lazar, who is legendary in book publishing. (See the Appendix for a list of the celebrities and brand names we have been associated with.)

The answer to the question, "How have you come to represent so many celebrities?" has to be, "Just bad luck."

Actually, it hasn't been that bad representing the greats and near greats, the famous and the infamous. As long as you realize that celebrities are just people you can get by, but it does take a special temperament to represent them. The most important thing is to understand that most celebrities require careful care and handling when it comes to their egos. When you are well known or truly famous you soon begin to believe that you are special.

The best definition of a celebrity that I can think of is "a celebrity is someone who, when he gets a traffic ticket for speeding after having had one drink too many, usually finds the story in the papers."

For you and me, receiving a traffic ticket for driving after a few martinis would probably go unnoticed except by the state trooper who gave us the ticket or the traffic magistrate who levied the fine.

Phil Donahue was a major coup for Bill Adler Books. For the last few years, whenever I have sat in on meetings with publicity people at publishing firms, the key question always has been, "Can we get the author on the "Donahue" program?"

One day after one of those meetings I suddenly thought, "I wonder if anybody has asked Donahue to write a book?" I decided to do just that.

I called Donahue in Chicago but was unable to get him on the phone. I called at least four times but with no luck. That didn't surprise me because obviously Donahue gets lots of phone calls and although I had told his secretary that I was a literary agent and wanted to talk to him about a book, it didn't make much of an impression.

I then decided to write Phil a letter and in the letter I mentioned some of the other authors I had represented, including Dan Rather and Mike Wallace. Little did I realize that Phil Donahue has enormous respect for both Rather and Wallace, but especially Mike whose interviewing technique he has always admired.

A few days after I wrote to Phil, I called him again. This time I got him on the phone. The conversation went something like this:

Adler: Phil, I'd like to talk to you about writing a book.

Donahue: I don't really know if I want to write a book.

Adler: Well, at least, I'd like to talk to you about it.

Donahue: I'm not even so sure that if I wrote a book I would have anything to say or if anybody would be interested.

Adler: Phil, you are wrong. Hundreds of thousands of people would be interested in your book.

Donahue: Well, I tell you what, Bill, next time you are going to be in Chicago, give me a ring and maybe we can get together.

Adler: It so happens, Phil, I'm going to be in Chicago tomorrow. (I had no intention of being in Chicago that next day.)

Donahue: You are? Well, okay, let's have lunch since you are going to be here anyway. As long as you're not making a special trip.

Phil and I agreed to meet for lunch at the Continental Plaza Hotel where I told Phil I would be staying. Luckily, my secretary was able to get a reservation there.

My lunch with Phil went well and I believe from the beginning that the chemistry between us was good.

The staff for the "Donahue" program is not large but it is a team-oriented organization. The executive producer, Dick Mincer, has been with the "Donahue" program since its first week in November 1967, as has Pat McMillen, the senior producer. Darlene Hayes, a producer, has been with the show eleven years and Sheri Singer, also a producer, joined the Donahue staff in 1974. Ron Weiner joined the show as director when the program moved from Dayton to Chicago, and so did Penny Rotheiser who handles the press relations. And last, but not least, is Lorraine Landelius, who has been Phil Donahue's secretary for the past six years.

It was toward the close of my lunch with Phil that he asked if I could stay over and meet with his staff the following day at the WGN studios.

"Of course, Phil," I eagerly replied. "No problem."

It was a problem. For one thing, the Continental Plaza Hotel and most of the other hotels were packed with one of the many conventions that always seem to be taking place in Chicago and for another, I had a full schedule the next day back in New York. But I had come this far and I had every intention of going all the way. I also sensed by the way Phil had indicated that he wanted me to meet his staff that if his staff didn't like me or the idea of Phil writing a book, he could easily be persuaded not to do it.

The next day I arrived at the studios of WGN just as Donahue was about to go off the air. Phil greeted me warmly, introduced me to his staff and suggested that we all go into a conference room to discuss my proposal that Phil write a book.

Book deals are made and lost sometimes in a second and often over a trivial matter. I know now that I almost lost the Donahue deal over something that at the time seemed trivial—my cigar.

I have been smoking cigars for years and they are a part of me. When the meeting started, I did what I have been doing at most meetings for the past twenty years, I lit up a cigar. Little did I realize that Pat McMillen not only hates cigars but they actually make her ill.

Not only is Pat the senior producer of Phil's program but she is a person Phil has come to rely on over the years and one whose judgment he respects. I am sure that if Pat had been against the idea of Phil writing a book or had not been in favor of the short, bald, bespectacled, cigar smoking agent, the prospects for a Donahue book would have been slim at best.

But Donahue and his staff did agree that the book was a good idea and gave me the mandate to find a publisher, and it was at that meeting that I learned the unusual details concerning the Donahue book.

Phil had decided that the book would be written in part by members of his staff and that he would share the advance and royalties from the book with them.

That generous (and fair) decision by Donahue was a financial windfall for his staff since the paperback rights alone to *Donahue* went to Fawcett for $1,633,640.

Donahue and his staff split that figure on a fifty-fifty basis with the hardcover publisher, Simon & Schuster, but when the paperback sale is added to the hardcover sale and the first serial sale to *Woman's Day* and to the book club sale to the Literary Guild, the amount due to the authors of *Donahue* was in excess of one million dollars.

The thought that a sixty-cent Don Diego cigar had almost cost me my 10% commission of $100,000 was almost enough to make me give up cigars forever.

Of all the celebrities I have represented, I think the question I've been asked most often is about Phil Donahue. "What is he really like?"

The answer simply stated is: "Donahue is bright, decent and concerned."

Phil Donahue is a hard-driving, restless, creative, inquisitive person who is probably more comfortable with newspaper reporters or television journalists than he is among movie stars. He is loyal to his staff and friends and has a good sense of humor.

It took about two years to have *Donahue by Donahue and Company* written, and during that entire period Phil and I really never had one angry word.

Donahue had originally planned to work with a professional writer on his book, but after about six months he decided to go it alone. That turned out to be a wise decision because Phil is a fine writer and his book was a good read, particularly because it sounded like him.

When the book was published in February 1980, Phil was very nervous. Phil was concerned about the reviews since most of the literary book reviewers are usually very hard on books written by show business types.

Phil did get good reviews except in the *New York Times*. I am convinced the reviewer had never seen the Donahue program or didn't know much about it or Phil's audience and really couldn't even begin to understand why Donahue was so popular or such a phenomenon.

The book was practically an instantaneous hit, and I think even Phil was a little surprised by its enormous success. Phil Donahue's book did far better than Merv Griffin's or Mike Douglas's autobiographies.

The reason?

The Donahue audience is loyal, intense and respectful of Phil and what he has to say and they are very curious about him. Merv, Mike and Phil all have an audience, but Phil really has a following.

There is one other thing that helped to make *Donahue* such a success: the book was honest and revelatory. For the most part, Phil did not pull any punches about his professional or personal life, and that's what his readers wanted. You can't simply put a celebrity's name on a book and expect it to sell unless there is something between the covers. That is a mistake publishers make all the time.

One of the biggest bombs in book publishing history was a disaster titled *Christmas with Ed Sullivan*, published at the height of Sullivan's popularity when he was "Mr. Sunday Night."

The equation has to be: Celebrity plus book that says something equals sales.

With all his success and fame, I'm sure Phil Donahue enjoyed the success of his book as much as, if not more than, anything else he has done personally or professionally.

Dan Rather's book, *The Camera Never Blinks*, was a book that wasn't supposed to have succeeded the way it did because at the time it was published Dan Rather was not the household name he is today.

Dan Rather is a no-nonsense journalist and yet the *real* Dan Rather is a concerned individual who always seems interested in people. That is the thing that has impressed me most about Rather. Recently my wife and daughter and I had dinner with Dan and his warm and delightful wife, Jean, and their handsome son, Dan, Jr., at David K's restaurant in New York. Rather spent a good part of the evening talking to our daughter, Diane, who is twenty-two, asking her questions and seeking out her opinions.

Rather is not just interested in Rather, and for a celebrity that is unusual, to say the least. Dan is a courteous and considerate person and, although I am sure he must at times lose his cool, I never saw him do so during the more than three years we worked together on *The Camera Never Blinks*.

There is a Yiddish word that perhaps best describes Rather. It is *mensch*—a real man in every sense of the word.

Cosell is one of my favorite celebrities.

I am now working on my third book with Howard Cosell, and I have enjoyed every minute of it.

Howard is brilliant. A graduate of New York University Law School, he was a successful attorney before he became a broadcaster. One of his clients as an attorney was Willie Mays.

At the Friars Club dinner we attended in honor of Burt Reynolds, Cosell was the wittiest speaker of the evening. He was sharper than Carson, who was master of ceremonies and funnier than Reynolds with timing that would put even Bob Hope to shame.

I love to tell the story of how I got Howard Cosell to write a book. Even though sports books or books by sports personalities are a big gamble, I knew that a book by Cosell would sell—and sell big. Cosell is the most dramatic and exciting sports journalist in the history of broadcast journalism or, for that matter, print journalism.

I didn't know Howard, but I called him up cold at ABC and asked him if we could have lunch. At the time I called Howard I wasn't aware that Random House had also called him to discuss a book. Over lunch with the Random House people, Howard was asked to put together an outline so that they could make an offer for his book. Cosell never did write the outline which didn't surprise me.

If you want to get a celebrity to write a book, it is a mistake to ask for an outline. Chances are he will never write one.

I lunched with Cosell at the Marmiton restaurant and a few minutes into our lunch, I asked Cosell if he were interested in writing a book.

"Maybe," he replied.

"I would like to do a book with you, Howard," I told him. "I think it would be a major bestseller."

Our luncheon continued and the subject of an outline never came up.

"If you are interested," Howard said as we were about to leave, "speak to Bob Schulman."

Bob Schulman, a former IRS agent, is one of the best and most successful accountants in Washington, D.C. He is the accountant for Edward Bennett Williams, the owner of the Washington Redskins, who is also one of the best-known attorneys in the country. Cosell, then as now, always kept good company.

The next day I spoke to Bob Schulman.

"Howard wants $100,000," Schulman told me pleasantly but directly. The year was 1972 and $100,000 for a sports book—even if it was by Howard Cosell—was a lot of money.

Howard was paid the $100,000 by Playboy Press.

Cosell was great to work with, a professional in every way, especially when it came to deadlines. I couldn't believe it when Howard delivered the manuscript for his book exactly on the day called for in his contract. Not a day earlier or a day later. And in the unreliable world of deadlines, that was truly remarkable.

I could never understand why publishers put delivery due dates in the contracts for books to be written by celebrities or stars. They are almost meaningless. I have under contract right now at least a dozen books by celebrities that are more than three years late. Although publishers are reluctant to wait three years beyond the delivery date for most writers to deliver a manuscript, they seem willing to wait for the celebrities.

Cosell by Cosell was an immediate hit and Howard enjoyed the success of his first published book.

We became close friends—Gloria and I and Howard and his bright, attractive wife, Emmy. Emmy is the real rock in Cosell's life. Without her, Howard would be a ship adrift, and he knows it.

It was on the basis of my friendship with him that Cosell agreed to write a second book, *Like It Is,* which was also published by Playboy Press.

Although *Like It Is* did better than 95 percent of the books published, it was not a national bestseller and looking back now the reason is clear.

The book was published a little over one year after Cosell's first book, and although the public was anxious for the first Cosell book, they were not so anxious to read the second one right away.

I take full blame for the decision to hurry into the writing of the second book because even Cosell was reluctant to take on the assignment, and Emmy was definitely not in favor of the second book at the time it was written.

Cosell's loyalty runs deep and now, seven years after the publication of *Like It Is,* we are working on our third book together to be published by Simon & Schuster.

I can't think of another celebrity who I have ever been with that gets the instant recognition or response that Cosell gets when he is either eating in a restaurant or just walking down the street. Everybody stops to talk to Cosell—not just to nod or say "hello" but usually to comment on something. People relate to Cosell. They respect his honesty and his candor.

The first time I met Nancy Reagan was in 1977 at her home in Pacific Palisades, a short drive from Beverly Hills.

Nancy is a lovely woman with fine features, beautiful eyes and a warm smile. She is also one of the most literate celebrities I have ever represented.

By literate, I don't mean in the literary sense of the word, but literate in the sense that if you tell Mrs. Reagan that you will have something ready on Tuesday, she expects it on Tuesday, not on Wednesday. It is not a question of being demanding; it is just that Nancy Reagan expects people to keep their word.

Actually, Ronald Reagan was my client before Nancy Reagan was. As in so many similar situations, Ronald Reagan became my client because of a chance dinner with another client of mine, Mike Wallace.

It was during a dinner in California with Mike that ex-governor and then private citizen, Ronald Reagan, mentioned to Wallace that he was thinking of writing a book. Wallace suggested that Reagan talk to me. Shortly after Mike returned to New York, I called Ronald Reagan at Mike's suggestion. I didn't get to talk to Reagan himself but rather his aide, Pete Hannaford, who is now also my client and has just completed a first-rate book about the Reagans. After a number of phone calls, a date was finally set for me to meet with Reagan in California.

Ronald Reagan is a nice person. That was my first and immediate impression of him. He was warm and friendly and he listened.

The book that Reagan wanted to write was about communism in Hollywood in the forties when Reagan was active in the Hollywood community and was president of the Screen Actors Guild.

I quickly sold the book (without an outline) to Michael Korda at Simon & Schuster.

When Reagan decided to run for the presidency, the direction of the book was changed to a book about Reagan's political philosophy—perhaps not so interesting an idea but certainly safe.

I remember the meeting with Reagan and Pete Hannaford in the study of Reagan's home in Pacific Palisades. The future president of the United States quickly agreed to changing the direction of the book and the entire conversation lasted no more than five minutes.

As I am writing this book, Ronald Reagan is still under contract to write his book for Simon & Schuster.

Reagan's book was late and once I received a rather terse phone call from Dick Snyder (the president of Simon & Schuster).

Snyder: Reagan's book is late.

Adler: I know, Dick.

Snyder: It's very late.

Adler: He's been busy campaigning.

Snyder: I think we should get our money back with interest.

Adler: Dick, why don't you wait until after the election? If he wins, you will have under contract the president of the United States and if he loses, you will have under contract the voice of the opposition. Remember after Barry Goldwater lost to Lyndon Johnson, he went on to write the bestseller, *The Conscience of a Conservative.*

Snyder: I'll think about it.

Dick never called me back and the question of the return of Ronald Reagan's advance was never raised again.

Shortly after I sold the book to Simon & Schuster for Ronald Reagan, I received a phone call from Pete Hannaford in California. "You did such a good job selling the book for Governor Reagan, how would you like to get a contract for Mrs. Reagan?"

I agreed to take on the assignment. I actually thought Nancy's book would sell better than her husband's because of its appeal to women.

Simon & Schuster was not interested in publishing Nancy Reagan's autobiography but Larry Hughes at William Morrow was, so Nancy signed with them.

One interesting sidelight on my representation of the Reagans had to do with their attorney, William French Smith, who is now the attorney general of the United States.

Gloria was particularly excited when I sold Ronald Reagan's book. She thought he was a very prestigious client.

I told Gloria not to get too excited since I was confident that once Reagan's attorney got hold of the contract, there wouldn't be any contract. I think all my life I am destined to be pessimistic about attorneys—especially in book publishing.

But the law offices of William French Smith surprised me. The changes they requested in both Ronald and Nancy's contracts were minimal. (About one-fourth of the changes requested by the attorney of a Midwestern disc jockey that I recently represented.)

A day or two after Reagan received the Republican nomination, Pete Hannaford was in my office. It was really just a social call but during the course of our conversation, I asked Pete if he would like to write a book about the Reagans.

Pete seemed mildly interested but was not convinced that he was the man to write a book about Reagan or if there would be a market for such a book.

"I think you are the man to write the book, Pete. First of all you have been an "insider" with Reagan for many years and secondly you can write," I told him.

Of all the Reagan intimates before he became president, Hannaford was the best writer and had written many of Reagan's speeches, including his acceptance speech at the Republican convention.

"There will be many books written about Reagan, Pete," I continued, "but most of them will be written by outsiders—newspaper reporters, political analysts—but you could be the first one who has been part of Reagan's inner circle to write a portrait of the Reagans."

Pete agreed it would be worth doing but the next question was, of course, could he get a contract. I was confident I could find a good publisher and a first-rate contract even though Hannaford hadn't written a word, and at that time Hannaford wasn't as well known in Washington and national circles as he is now, thanks, in part, to the celebrated Richard Allen/Nancy Reagan/Japanese article donnybrook.

The next morning I called Larry Hughes at Morrow and he asked for a day to think about it. He called back to say he wasn't interested. I then called Jack Geoghegan who at the time was chairman of Coward, McCann & Geoghegan (part of the Putnam Publishing Group). Jack has since left Coward, McCann and by coincidence is now working for Larry Hughes at William Morrow as a senior editor-at-large.

Geoghegan was more than mildly interested but he first asked the right question.

"Suppose Reagan loses?" Jack said. "What happens then? I agree that if Reagan becomes president, a book by Hannaford could have a shot."

"Jack," I replied, "let's draft a contract with two different advances. If Reagan wins, then Hannaford will receive X number of dollars. If Reagan should lose then Hannaford will receive an advance of X number of dollars less 50%. Even if Reagan loses, there will be a market for an 'insider's book' about the Reagans, but it will probably be worth the 50% left."

"Okay," Jack said, "you've got a deal but only if Hannaford will start writing right away."

"That's exactly why I want to make the deal now, Jack," I told him, "so Pete can start work now whether Reagan wins or not."

As things turned out, it was a profitable election for Pete because the advance for his book was X dollars not X minus 50%.

I must admit it was one of the most unusual publishing deals we had ever made.

Nancy Reagan needed a collaborator for her book and that always presents a difficult problem. Finding a collaborator to work with a celebrity is similar to being a professional matchmaker. Your chances of success are problematical. Sometimes you do get lucky, but every time I put a writer together with a well-known person, I hold my breath.

In selecting a writer I take into consideration not only the writer's talents and ability but also his or her talent for getting along with the celebrity—almost as important as the writing skills.

In the case of Nancy Reagan, my first choice was a writer who had worked well with other celebrities and who had a low-key personality that I thought would fit with Mrs. Reagan.

I was right and wrong.

Nancy liked the writer but after the first few chapters, she didn't like the job he had done. But what impressed me about Mrs. Reagan was her concern for the sensitivity of the writer. "I feel so badly," she told me. "I don't want to hurt his feelings."

I assured Mrs. Reagan that the writer was a professional and that professionals understand these things. The writer did understand and was paid fairly for his work.

Bill Libby, the next writer to collaborate with the future First Lady, worked out fine. Libby is a first-rate collaborator and we have done many books together, including James Roosevelt's book about his parents and Gale Storm's autobiography.

Nancy did all right but not as well as we had hoped. I had always thought that Mrs. Reagan could have written a stronger book, but taking everything into consideration she wrote what was the right book for her at the time considering that her husband was running for president just about the time the book was published.

It turned out to be very difficult to promote the book during the presidential campaign. Most of the important television programs could not have Mrs. Reagan on to promote her book because if they had, they would have had to give equal time to the other candidates' wives even though they hadn't written books.

It was also difficult to coordinate Mrs. Reagan's book promotion schedule with her political schedule so the net of all of this was that *Nancy* by Nancy Reagan was not a bestseller.

Mickey Herskowitz may be one of the best collaborators working today. Together, Herskowitz and I have done a score of collaborations. I say together although I had the easy job—he had to write them.

Herskowitz has written and I have represented books with Jimmy the Greek, Gene Autry, Gene Tierney, George Blanda, Dan Rather and Mark Spitz. Most recently, Herskowitz is working on Bette Davis's autobiography.

Mickey Herskowitz has great charm, warmth, talent and a marvelous sense of humor. When it came time to select a writer to work with Bette Davis, she was insistent on a woman.

I pleaded with Howard Cady, the editor at William Morrow to at least let Bette Davis meet Mickey. (I didn't represent Bette Davis. She is represented by Robbie Lantz.) Cady consented although he didn't hold out much hope since Miss Davis was so positive she wanted to work only with a woman.

One meeting with Mickey and it was love at first sight. From the very beginning they got along famously, as I knew they would.

There is always a question as to whether a collaborator should receive credit on the book jacket for his or her efforts or remain anonymous.

I prefer to give the writer full credit on the title page reading, "by Nancy Reagan with Bill Libby" or "by Bess Myerson and Bill Adler" as when I collaborated with Bess on *The I Love New York Diet.*

The financial split between the writer and the celebrity depends on a number of factors, the most important of which is the size of the advance, since that helps determine the amount of money available for the writer to write the book. In most instances, it is the writer or collaborator who needs the lion's share of the advance in order to have enough money to research and write the book.

The split on royalties also depends on the collaborator and how successful he or she has been in the past.

Mickey Herskowitz receives 50% of the royalties as does, I assume, A. E. Hotchner, who co-authored the bestsellers by Doris Day and Sophia Loren.

Mike Wallace is an old friend of mine; we met more than twenty-five years ago when I was program director for the Channel 5 television station in New York. Mike was just beginning what has become his trademark—"the Mike Wallace interview" with his "Nightbeat" program.

I first proposed to Mike that he write his autobiography in 1977 when I met him on the Eastern Airlines shuttle flying from Washington to New York.

Mike was reluctant. "Maybe when I retire," Mike said.

"Mike," I told TV's premier interviewer, "when you retire nobody will care. Memories are very short in your business."

Mike still wasn't convinced but suggested that Gloria and I have dinner with him and his wife, Lorraine, to discuss the possibility further.

I have learned that when it comes to the decision of writing an autobiography, the spouse is an important factor. I knew I would have to convince Lorraine if I had any sort of chance of convincing Mike.

Lorraine Wallace is a fine woman, lovely to look at and to be with and a very talented artist. (As a matter of fact, one of her paintings hangs in our living room.) Lorraine seemed to be in favor of the book as we talked that night over dinner at the Four Seasons, but she kept repeating that Mike is really a very private person despite his public image.

Obviously, if Mike Wallace was going to write his autobiography, it would not be for the money involved since Mike, like Cosell and Rather and others, is financially secure, but rather because it would be nice to leave behind a document that would permanently record a career he was proud of.

Mike decided to write his autobiography and shortly after the decision was made, the book was bought by Dick Snyder at Simon & Schuster.

At first, Mike decided he would need a collaborator. Mike was very busy traveling around the world for "60 Minutes" and he was not too sure he would have the time to write his book alone.

We selected Neil Offen, a fine young writer, to work with Mike, and they spent many hours together taping Mike's story. But when Offen submitted the first draft of Mike's book, Mike was not exactly thrilled.

Mike Wallace is one of the most direct people I know. He says what he thinks and he says it quickly. In this case, he decided that if he were going to write his autobiography he would have to do it himself. And that is exactly what he set out to do.

For at least six months, Mike worked on his book and it seemed to be going well, but then suddenly Mike decided he didn't want to write the book at all. What bothered Mike the most were the personal things that would have to be in an autobiography. He just didn't want to write about them and he was equally convinced that his own story was not that exciting.

I was depressed. I really wanted Mike to write his book because I was sure it would be a major bestseller.

A few weeks after Mike gave me the upsetting news that he wasn't going ahead, he called me at home on a Saturday morning. "I have an idea," Mike said. "Suppose instead of my autobiography, I write a book about my television years of interviewing people. What do you think?"

In half an hour I was over at Mike's brownstone and we were talking about the book. "It's a great idea, Mike," I told him, "especially if you write the stories behind some of your most important interviews like Begin, Sadat, Haldeman, Reagan, Elsa Maxwell, Mike Quill, Al Capp, Drew Pearson, Tallulah Bankhead, Frank Lloyd Wright and the many, many celebrities you have interviewed."

Mike was enthusiastic and so was I. Essentially Mike's story revolved around his twenty-five years as an interviewer and journalist so it made sense to build the book that way. But most important of all, Mike could write his book without making it a typical autobiography.

I met with Simon & Schuster and presented the plans for Mike's book since, of course, they had contracted for Mike's autobiography.

Michael Korda expressed mild enthusiasm for the new book and Dick Snyder shared his cool reaction. "We would be happy to publish twenty-five years of Mike Wallace interviews," Korda told me, "but not for the same advance we were willing to pay for his autobiography. We think it is worth less money."

As so often happens in this business, I was able to sell *Twenty-five Years of Mike Wallace Interviews* to William Morrow and Mike is now collaborating with Gary Gates, a fine writer and journalist.

You can never tell where a celebrity book will come from.

During the presidential election that brought Jimmy Carter to the White House in 1976, Kandy Stroud, a writer I was representing, was covering Carter in Plains, Georgia. Kandy had the opportunity to get to know the Carter family, including Gloria Carter Spann, Jimmy Carter's oldest sister.

Gloria Carter Spann approached Kandy in Plains and asked her how she should go about getting published a collection of her mother's letters that had been written while "Miss Lillian" was serving in the Peace Corps in India from 1966 to 1968.

Kandy asked me if I would be interested and I said I was. I called Gloria Carter Spann in Plains and she briefly described the content of her mother's letters to me.

Since at the time everybody was assuming that Jimmy Carter was going to be the next president of the United States, I knew that virtually anything written by his mother would result in a substantial book contract.

I wasn't wrong.

The next day a phone call to Joni Evans at Simon & Schuster resulted in a $35,000 contract for Gloria Carter Spann who was to be the editor of *Away from Home: Letters to My Family.*

The book did fairly well and the paperback rights were purchased by Warner Books.

There are two interesting sidelights in connection with that book.

Although I had sold the book and had many phone conversations with Gloria Carter Spann, we had never met.

One day shortly before the book had been completed, I had a phone conversation with Mrs. Spann that went something like this:

Gloria Spann: Bill, can I ask you a question?

Adler: Sure.

Gloria Spann: You won't mind?

Adler: No.

Gloria Spann: Are you black or white?

At first I was surprised by Gloria's question and then I thought of my son or daughter who would probably have replied that it was none of her business. But I quickly decided that this wasn't the time to get into a philosophical discussion so I replied, "Gloria, I am white."

I really shouldn't have been stunned by Gloria Carter Spann's question. Perhaps it seemed to her in Plains, Georgia that a good portion of the people in Manhattan must be black. I don't think the question was meant as a racial slur but it certainly was an unusual remark coming from the sister of the man who was about to become the leader of the free world.

Shortly after that phone conversation, my wife and I had to go down to Plains to meet with Gloria to discuss some details in connection with the book that couldn't be discussed over the phone. Gloria and her husband, Walter, met us at the airport. As we were driving to Plains, Gloria turned to me.

"Bill," she said, "can I ask you a question?"

She already knew I was white.

"Sure," I replied.

"Are you a Jew?"

"Yes, Gloria," I told her. "I'm Jewish."

"Good," Gloria responded. "I'd rather have a Jew handle my business than a Baptist."

My first celebrity book involved Margaret Truman.

I had an idea for a book called *White House Pets* which would be about all the pets that lived with presidential families in the White House. I realized that I needed someone to work on the book who could help to make it more than just a book about dogs, cats, horses, goats and the White House.

Margaret Truman was perfect for the book. As the daughter of the thirty-third president of the United States, she not only had lived in the White House but she was an active, visible, well-liked personality. I was able to present the idea to Margaret and, although I later discovered she wasn't really crazy about pets, she agreed to collaborate with me on the book.

White House Pets was not a very successful book but it did lead to a book that became the number one bestseller in the country.

Shortly after *White House Pets* was published, I suggested to Margaret that she write, with the assistance of a professional writer, a book about her father. Margaret wasn't convinced that such a book would sell but I persisted and we sold the book to Larry Hughes at William Morrow.

The book did become a major hit and it obviously rode the crest of the wave of renewed interest in President Truman and his new popularity as one of the most respected presidents of the twentieth century.

Even to this day, I can't understand why Margaret resisted all efforts by the publisher and myself to persuade her to title the book, *My Father*. Margaret insisted on titling the book *Harry S. Truman* which wasn't as close or warm a title as *My Father*. But the title obviously didn't affect sales.

We have developed many books like *White House Pets* by Margaret Truman where we have matched the celebrity with the idea. The books have included:

Yes, You Can! by Art Linkletter (An inspirational book on how you can succeed in business.)

Public Speaking for Private People by Art Linkletter

Pray to Win by Pat Boone

How to Survive in Your Business and Your Personal Life by Dick Clark

Looking Great, Staying Young by Dick Clark

Lorne Greene's *Book of Remarkable Animals*

A Special Kind of Courage by Geraldo Rivera

My Secrets of Playing Baseball by Willie Mays

Women of Courage by Margaret Truman

Over 40: Feeling Great by George Blanda

Buster Crabbe's Arthritis Exercise Book

The celebrity book is a growing category as more and more publishers discover that very few books can attract the sort of attention from the media and the public that a book written by a celebrity does.

Today Bill Adler Books, Inc. is representing celebrity books in the process of being written by Jessica Savitch, Willard Scott, Joan Lunden, Larry King, Robert MacNeil, Bob Keeshan (Captain Kangaroo), Charles Osgood, Morton Dean, Ron Nessen, Nancy Reagan, Mike Wallace, Irving Mansfield, Paul Sorvino, Steve Allen, Howard Cosell, Dr. Lee Salk and William Rusher.

The Ins and the Outs

DIET books are in (*The Beverly Hills Diet,* the *Never-Say-Diet Book, The Scarsdale Diet* and the *I Love New York Diet*). Books about meditation and ESP that were so big only a few years ago are out.

Saturday Review has been out for a few years and still is, but the *New York Times Book Review* is still in despite the fact that it frequently reviews the most obtuse books that appeal to maybe sixty people—probably sixty people who work at the *New York Times.*

Books about running have about run their course and if Jim Fixx were to write *The Complete Book of Running* today he would probably sell a few thousand copies instead of the 855,721 copies sold when the book was published in 1978.

Celebrity autobiographies are in. Look at the bestseller sales of Shelley Winters, Ingrid Bergman, Lauren Bacall, Sophia Loren and Doris Day.

Books about the women's movement are about as popular today as Phyllis Schlafly is with women who are in favor of ERA.

Religious inspirational books are weak and books about the joys of living alone or being single are in.

Dick Snyder, the president of Simon & Schuster is in, and so is Larry Hughes at William Morrow. William Jovanovich is out although he is still in power.

Joseph Heller is out but John Irving is in. Avery Corman was never quite in although for somebody who made a lot of money, it is surprising that he never really was.

Promoting your book on the "John Davidson" program is out but appearing on "Donahue" is still definitely in.

"Good Morning America" is in and so is the "Today" show and Larry King but Mike Douglas is not.

Doubleday is still big but not really in, but The Linden Press is. Joni Evans, the publisher of The Linden Press, is definitely in.

Ace Books is "iffy" and NAL is not in. Pocket Books and its president, Ron Busch, are in and the new line of romance novels, Silhouette Books, are solid and in.

Marc Jaffe at Random House/Ballantine Books is still in but not superagent Swifty Lazar who will soon be out of movie stars to represent.

Jackie Applebaum, the bright young publicist who handled the publicity for *The Beverly Hills Diet,* is in and undoubtedly her fees have gone up.

Edwin McDowell, the publishing columnist for the *New York Times,* seems to be more in than some of his predecessors and Don Fine at Arbor House is still going strong.

Multimillion-dollar paperback deals are out but middle six-figure advances are still in for the big books.

Norman Mailer is out but Robert Lindsey, author of *The Falcon and the Snowman,* is in and will be even more in as time goes on.

Crown Publishers are sort of in but not as in as they were when they published *Scruples.*

Bernard Geis is coming back and may be back in again. It's doubtful if Grosset & Dunlap which was never really in will ever be.

Jim Silberman, the president of Summit Books, is in and probably always will be.

Book reviews in *Time* magazine are out but a paragraph in *People Magazine* is in.

Conglomerates in book publishing are out (or at least many of them would like to be) and so are foreign publishers who own American publishing firms.

Trade paperbacks are in and so is Jim Landis who is publisher of trade paperbacks at William Morrow.

Jack Artenstein, president of the trade paperback division at Simon & Schuster, is in.

Appearing on the "700 Club" is in and so is Sherry Arden at William Morrow.

Books that tell women how to enjoy sex, be aggressive in business and learn to love their mothers are out (thank goodness) but confessions of alcoholics or drug addicts are coming back.

Autobiographies by "jocks" are still out and so are books about tennis and golf, but cookbooks that tell how to prepare food simply and purely are big.

Books telling the "truth" about dead celebrities are in, but sex books are fading—enough is enough.

Allan Barnard at Bantam is in because he has lasted so long and so is Phyllis Grann at Putnam's because she is so good.

Jack Geoghegan was out for about two weeks but he is coming back and John Dodds is in again at William Morrow.

Book reviews in *Publishers Weekly* are out because nobody in the industry pays much attention but the *Kirkus* reviews are in—probably because they hardly ever like a book.

Books about the Moral Majority are in and will sell.

Workman Publishing may be the most in of all the publishers and Prentice-Hall may be the one that is the most out.

Being mentioned on "Page Six" of the *New York Post* used to be in when Claudia Cohen was writing the column, but now that James Brady is editing "Page Six," it is out.

Liz Smith is big but an appearance on "Live at Five" is out because they will take practically anybody.

It looked for a while as if David Obst would really be in, but he has faded and so has Larry Schiller, the book packager who put together the Lenny Bruce and Marilyn Monroe books.

Delilah Books is in and getting big. J.P. Tarcher looked like he might really be in but that hasn't come to pass.

Bob Gottlieb at Knopf is still in and, like Jim Silberman, probably always will be. Sol Stein at Stein & Day was in for a few years but not now.

Lyle Stuart seems to be in every other year and the National Book Awards are still out.

The Frankfurt Book Fair is in because nobody can think of a better substitute and the ABA Convention is out because it is a lot of effort without much result.

16

The Money Places

MORE publishing deals are made over lunch, dinner, cocktails and breakfast in book publishing than in most businesses. Scott Meredith never goes out to lunch (although he does have business dinners) but Scott is the exception.

Lunch is very big in book publishing. Morton Janklow usually sits at the same table in the bar room at the Four Seasons and many other publishing heavyweights have their own favorite and permanent tables at the Four Seasons such as Michael Korda, Patricia Soliman, Eleanor Rawson and Betty Prashker. Other regulars for lunch, drinks and dinner include Gladys Carr, Howard Kaminsky, Lenore Hershey and Joni Evans.

The Four Seasons, owned and managed by Tom Margittai and Paul Kovi, is *the* publishing restaurant. If Margittai and Kovi were ever cut in on only a small percentage of the deals made in their handsome restaurant, they wouldn't have to work another day.

A few years ago I sold a novel to Jonathan Dolger when he was a senior editor at Harper & Row. The novel was called *The Restaurant* and was to be a fictionalized version of the Four Seasons. Paul Kovi and Tom Margittai had agreed to work with a novelist on the book to add authenticity to the story but at the last minute Tom and Paul decided not to go ahead with the book fearing, I suspect, that some of their better customers would not be in favor of them writing a book about the people who frequent the Four Seasons, even if it was fiction.

It is easy to feel at home at the Four Seasons because they go out of their way to make you feel that way, and publishing people especially like to go there because that is where they can meet and greet and see and be seen by other publishing people. In addition, the food at the Four Seasons is some of the best served in New York.

Most people in book publishing like the bar room at the Four Seasons but I prefer the pool room where I usually sit at the same table.

There are other in and popular luncheon places in Manhattan for publishing people. The Madrigal restaurant is a favorite of Ellis Amburn, Phyllis Grann, Lenore Hershey, George Walsh, and Herb Katz. Joni Evans and Linda Grey are regulars at San Marco. Le Perigord attracts many in the publishing industry such as Larry Hughes, Phyllis Grann and Ellis Amburn, and the Century Club has Evan Thomas and Lenore Hershey. Raga is a favorite of Joni Evans, Gladys Carr and Ron Busch.

Joanna, Cafe Loup, 65 Irving Place and the Dardanelles are favorite haunts of Roger Straus and the editors at Farrar, Straus & Giroux.

La Petite Marmite has such regulars as Ellis Amburn, Larry Hughes and many of the Dell and Doubleday editors. Rob Fitz is a steady customer at Shezan and La Colombe d'Or is a favorite of Sherry Arden and Mike Cohn. Howard Kaminsky can be found at "21," Pearl's and La Hosteria. The King Cole Room counts Gladys Carr and Herb Katz as patrons. Linda Grey can be found at La Côte Basque.

The most popular breakfast place in book publishing is the Brasserie which is located just the other side of the Seagram Building from the Four Seasons. I personally enjoy doing business at the Brasserie for breakfast and the Four Seasons for lunch. The Brasserie even provides free copies of the *New York Times* and the *Wall Street Journal.*

Whenever I have breakfast at the Brasserie I always meet someone else from publishing there like Bob Stein, the editor-in-chief at *McCalls* magazine, or Victor Temkin who is the president of Berkley Books. Incidentally, the cheese danish at the Brasserie is the best in New York.

I have made many deals over breakfast, lunch, dinner or cocktails but my favorite one involves a book that I thought of as I was walking over to have dinner with a major publisher at one of his favorite restaurants, the Four Seasons.

At the time, isometric exercise books were very popular and the thought occurred to me that there could be a commercial book on how to exercise while you were watching television at home.

I waited until we'd had a drink and although the purpose of our dinner was to discuss some of the books we were doing together, I mentioned the idea to the publisher. "Good idea," the publisher responded after I presented a brief description. "Let's do it."

"Great," I replied. "How about an advance of $10,000 which I think is a fair price."

"Agreed," the publisher said and we went on with the rest of our evening.

A few days later, I had the book contract. It was a profitable dinner for me and the publisher, and although the book was not a resounding success, the advance was small enough so that the publisher was able to make a profit as did Bill Adler Books.

If you are going to close a deal at breakfast, lunch or dinner then you have to be talking across the table to someone who can close a deal on the spot without checking with someone else. It can be pleasant and perhaps even fruitful to break bread or have a scotch with a senior editor or the editor-in-chief of a publishing firm, but it is far better to be with the man or woman who doesn't have to check with anyone.

A number of years ago, I was hired by Prentice-Hall to work as a writer with Richard Ettinger, the co-founder and chief executive of that major textbook and financial services publishing firm. (The trade publishing division of Prentice-Hall has always been a small part of their publishing operation.)

During the course of tape recording Ettinger's memoirs, I asked him why he had never moved the Prentice-Hall trade division to New York from Englewood Cliffs, New Jersey where the Prentice-Hall corporate headquarters were located. "It seems to me," I told him, "that your trade editors should be in Manhattan where most of the agents are located."

"I don't want my trade editors in Manhattan because I don't want them wasting three hours at lunch every day," Ettinger replied.

He may have had a point.

The fact is that the lunch ritual is at least two and a half hours long, and it is virtually impossible to get any editor on the phone from noon until three o'clock.

Most editors would rather be shot than be without a lunch date and only a few days ago an editor at a major publishing firm asked if I could have lunch with him.

"Sure," I replied. "When do you want to do it?"

"Well," the editor told me, "how about November 25? That's my first open date."

I wouldn't have minded the November 25 date but at the time of the phone call, it was October 5.

"Look," I told the editor, "November 25 is a long time away and I may be out of town in late November. Why don't you give me a call when you have an open date a little sooner?"

I wasn't playing hard to get. It was just that I find the ritual of scheduling lunches two months in advance a little silly. But that's the way it is done in book publishing.

One of the minor advantages of being an agent is that unless you are taking a client out for a meal, you almost never have to pick up the check. The rules of the publishing game are such that editors and publishers pay for the breakfast, lunch, dinner and drinks for the agent. I guess that if you were a successful agent with top-flight clients you could dine for the rest of your professional career without picking up a check.

If the IRS ever diabolically changes the rules involving business meals, the publishing industry will have to find a whole new way of conducting much of its business; but in the meantime in order to remain trim and thin in book publishing, you either have to jog a lot between meals or order salads most of the time.

Twenty-Four Good Book Ideas

HERE, in no particular order, are twenty-four book ideas (fiction and nonfiction) that I think are good ones and perhaps, in some cases, bestselling ideas. Obviously, the idea is only the starting point. In order for a good book idea to succeed, the execution of the idea is as important as the idea itself.

Some of the ideas for books I am presenting here may require the assistance of an expert (medical or otherwise), but all these ideas are doable and publishable.

Incidentally, I am stating here and now in black and white that these ideas are for free. There is no percentage or fee required for Bill Adler Books. These ideas are a bonus for those writers, editors, publishers or anyone else who had the good judgment to purchase this book.

1. A nonfiction book about the positive effects of tension. Much has been written about the negative effects of tension and how it can raise your blood pressure, give you migraine headaches and make you more prone to heart attacks, but many medical people feel that tension (in moderate amounts) can act as a stimulant and help you to be more creative and successful.

2. *The Last American President*. A novel about a military takeover in the United States and the end of democracy in the U.S.A.

3. *Weekend Sex: How to Make the Most of It*. For a large percen-

tage of Americans, especially those who have been married for a while, sex is confined to the weekend. Saturday and Sunday aren't always the best or the most romantic times to make love, so *Weekend Sex* would be a book dedicated to showing you how to get the most out of lovemaking during that brief period of time.

4. *A Traveler's Guide for Nonsmokers*. There are millions of people today who not only have given up smoking but are fanatics about not being around people who smoke on planes, trains, hotels, restaurants, etc. *Traveler's Guide for Nonsmokers* would list all the facilities in the major airports, trains and hotels around the world and the rules and regulations that favor the nonsmoker.

5. *Your First Investment*. A basic book on investing in the stock market for young people. Everything the first investor should know about stocks, bonds, mutual funds, stockbrokers, etc., all written in simple, concise language so that it can easily be understood by young people or, for that matter, adults who are ready to make their first investment.

6. *An Unauthorized Biography of Cary Grant*. Grant is one of the last of the great movie stars from the golden age of Hollywood. Not only has he had one of the greatest movie careers but he has had a complicated and controversial personal life.

7. A novel about a modern day Jack the Ripper who terrorizes a small American city like Muncie, Indiana.

8. *The Wine Diet*. How you can enjoy the pleasures of drinking wine and still lose weight and maintain your weight loss while drinking wine with your meals.

9. *An Examination of Dwight D. Eisenhower as a Military Man*. Much has been written about Eisenhower, the man and the president, but there haven't been many good books (and certainly not recently) about the man who rose quickly from being a relatively unimportant one-star general to Supreme Commander of all Allied Forces during World War II.

10. A science fiction novel about a new generation of domestic cats that plots to take over the earth because of supernatural powers. What could be more terrifying than kittens and cats who have the power to control the world?

11. *How Ex-Presidents Make a Living*. Although the book would need a jazzier title, it could be a fascinating and commercial idea. Former presidents have made livings in some strange ways, and Americans con-

tinue to have a fascination with their presidents whether in or out of office, alive or dead. Old presidents don't just fade away. Some of them go on to make a few dollars.

12. *The Second Child.* A book for parents on what to expect when there is more than one child in the family. The arrival of a second child always brings problems for the parents—how to let the first child know you still love him or her, how to deal with the feelings of competition between the older and younger child and so on.

13. *Weekend Jobs: How to Get One.* This book would map out ways anyone can successfully get a weekend job to make that much-needed extra money. I think this book should probably be a trade paperback but certainly in today's inflationary economy with everybody except the rich needing extra income, this book could sell.

14. A novel about an attractive woman in her late thirties who becomes the most powerful person in the banking world and quickly builds her own financial empire. Although on the surface such a woman would appear to have everything, she is actually a lonely, unhappy woman who experiments with everything from drugs to sex in her desperate search for some happiness to go along with her billions.

This is also a novel about the behind-the-scenes wheeling and dealing in the financial capitals of the world.

15. *Back-R-Cize.* An exercise book specifically designed to help people with bad backs—and that means practically everybody now and then. It would be a good idea to have an expert for this book, a physical fitness instructor or a doctor or both.

16. *The Final Superbowl* (A satirical novel). Many people, and I happen to be one of them, feel that sports mania is out of control in the United States and that Americans spend much too much money and time on sports. The idea for this novel is therefore about an amendment to the Constitution (or a law) that is proposed that would ban all sports in the U.S. because they are seriously affecting our moral fiber and intellectual capacity.

This would be a difficult novel to write but in the hands of someone with a sense of humor it could be a successful novel, not to mention a funny motion picture. I hope Cosell will forgive me for this idea.

17. *How to Promote Yourself.* One of the most important attributes for succeeding in business and in life is the ability to promote yourself with your boss, your colleagues, etc. If you don't know how to blow your own horn, it is doubtful that you will succeed at all. Obviously,

there are people who have made it without self-promotion but they are rare.

The book doesn't really need an expert but should be written by somebody who has made it and for whom self-promotion has played a role in his or her success.

This book needs a catchy, "come-on" title that captures the spirit of the book and offers a promise.

18. If you want to write a nonfiction book on a controversial subject, I couldn't think of a better one than the Moral Majority. A book that directs itself to the question, "the Moral Majority, is it a force for good or evil?" should sell.

No group since the women's liberation movement has caused as much furor as the Moral Majority and the controversy is more than likely to be with us for a long time to come.

19. *The Perfect Marriage*. Nothing is on the increase more than divorce and some marriages are splitting before the parties involved have even had the chance to open their wedding gifts. Why not a book about marriages that work and not just new marriages but marriages that have worked after five, ten, fifteen, twenty-five years and beyond. What are those elements and characteristics that make some marriages succeed while others fail?

The Perfect Marriage should be based on interviews with people whose marriages have worked and should be written by a psychiatrist or a marriage counselor who has clinical knowledge of marriages that have succeeded and why.

20. *The Brothers*. A novel set in New York at the turn of the century about three young men, one Irish, one Italian and one Jewish who grew up in the same neighborhood and were so close that they started a club that they called "The Brothers."

The Brothers follows the three young men and the generations that come after them against a backdrop of New York from the turn of the century to the 1980s.

21. *The Divorce Personality*. A number of years ago there was a very successful book about the types of personalities that would be most prone to having a heart attack. If you had the Type A personality, then you were more likely to have a heart attack than Type B or Type C.

I have an idea for a book that would use the same approach to analyze various types in terms of which personality types are most likely to have a divorce. This is a book someone would buy *before* getting married.

The Divorce Personality should be written with an expert in the field of marriage or perhaps even a psychiatrist or clinical psychologist.

22. *Growing Up Safe*. One of the things that concerns parents most is the safety of their children. Injuries to children can cause anguish and pain.

It isn't just physical injuries that worry parents. It is the other factors such as a child's taking the wrong medication or taking too much medication, a boating or swimming accident, or a mishap that occurs when a child plays with a pet. There are a thousand ways that young children can injure or hurt themselves, and *Growing Up Safe* would be a no-nonsense common sense book for parents on how they can minimize the chances of injuries to their children.

23. *An Unauthorized Biography of Jesse Helms.* Jesse Helms is one of the most important men in the United States Senate. Helms's power comes from the fact that he is the spokesperson for the Moral Majority in the Senate and, as such, speaks not only for himself and his constituents from North Carolina but for millions of Americans who believe in the principles of the Moral Majority. When Jesse Helms speaks, the Senate and the president of the United States listen.

Helms' story could be a fascinating book and one that I think would sell. I doubt if the senator would cooperate on such a book, but an unauthorized book would probably be even more interesting since it could include material that perhaps Helms would rather not talk about and since unauthorized biographies are usually not as self-serving as the authorized kind.

24. *Everything You've Always Wanted to Know about Money but Didn't Know Who to Ask*. Money books, if done well, can have a good market—especially in these times.

Everything You've Always Wanted to Know about Money but Didn't Know Who to Ask is a first-rate title for a money book. The book should be written in a question-and-answer format and should cover everything from what to know about bank interest to securing mortgage loans to mutual funds and even to investing abroad.

A financial expert would be necessary for this book.

18

The Twenty Questions People Ask Me Most about Publishing

1. Do you have to know somebody or have a connection to get a book published?

It's not essential but it is difficult to get a publisher to pay attention or take any interest in your proposed book if you are approaching him cold. A contact within a publishing firm—even if it is only someone in the mailroom—will help to get an editor to look at your manuscript or book proposal.

Many books that have arrived at publishing firms unsolicited have been published but the odds are against you. If you want to be published and you don't know anyone in publishing, call everyone you know until you find someone who knows an employee of a publishing house.

2. Are publishers honest?

Ninety-nine out of one hundred book publishers are honest and pay their royalties in a fair and honest manner. There are, of course, some exceptions, but you can be reasonably sure that if a publisher has been around for a while he is honest—especially publishers that belong to the Association of American Publishers.

Virtually all publishing contracts give the author the right to audit the publisher's books but in all my years in publishing, I have never found it to be necessary.

3. How can you get an agent to represent you?

It's easier to get some agents to take on your book properties than others. Obviously, some of the superagents are difficult to get to. But most of the young agents and even some of the better-known and established agents will be willing to look at your material. Whether they will take it on depends, of course, on the material.

The best approach is to write a one-page letter to the agent describing the project and follow up with a phone call. Never send a letter written in longhand to an agent or, for that matter, to a publisher. Borrow a typewriter if you have to, but get the letter typed.

4. How long should a book be?

Long enough to cover the subject. Most first-time authors are overly concerned with the length of a book. The average number of words for most books published today is between 80,000 and 100,000 words, but there have been many successful books that have had as few as 15,000 words that have covered the subject.

A book that is too long is, in my judgment, a mistake. This is especially true today because books are so expensive to produce. The days when books were 150,000 or 200,000 words are gradually coming to an end. There have been too many books that have been unnecessarily long.

5. How can I get my book reviewed?

No one should put pressure on a newspaper or a magazine or a book reviewer. It might even be counterproductive. Reviewers don't like to be pressed but if you have reason to believe that a particular newspaper or magazine or reviewer doesn't have a copy of your book to review because the publisher didn't send a copy then you certainly should do so.

Most publishers automatically send out review copies to their list of book reviewers but not every publisher is efficient in this area. The best policy (and the wisest) for an author is to double-check with the publisher if he is concerned that a particular reviewer hasn't received a copy. But don't send a note or make a phone call to reviewers asking them to review the book. That's a big mistake.

6. What is the biggest mistake most authors make?

Putting too much trust in publishers on the assumption that they will do everything right.

Publishers are human and so are editors. You must follow up yourself with the publisher on most aspects of the publishing process—especially promotion. Don't count on anything and, short of making yourself a pain for the publisher, keep on top of things. Your job isn't over when you finish writing the book. It has just started.

7. Why do some books succeed while others fail dismally?

The first reason is the quality of the manuscript, whether it is fiction or nonfiction.

Many books that either aren't very good or don't receive very good reviews do succeed, however.

Certainly Judith Krantz hasn't received acclaim from most reviewers and neither has Harold Robbins or Irving Wallace, yet their books have all been major bestsellers.

But for most books it is important that they, at the very least, be "good reads." Luck and timing certainly play a role in the success of any book and subject matter is equally important.

Promotion is the cornerstone of success in book publishing, and if a book is going to sell more than 2,000 copies there has to be sufficient creative advertising and promotion behind the book.

8. If you don't receive a big advance for your book, doesn't it mean that the publisher won't get behind the book?

If a publisher pays an advance of $100,000 for a book, then he is obviously going to have to get behind the book with advertising and promotion because he has such a big investment in it.

However, for many of the major bestsellers that I have been involved with either as agent or author or packager, the advances have been considerably less than $100,000 and yet the books were very successful.

Those books include *Harry S. Truman* by Margaret Truman, *The Camera Never Blinks* by Dan Rather and Mickey Herskowitz, *The Kennedy Wit, Letters from Camp, Donahue, The Relaxation Response* by Dr. Herbert Benson, *Full Disclosure* by William Safire, *Pills That Don't Work* by Dr. Sidney Wolfe, *Diet for Life* by Francine Prince and *The I Love New York Diet,* to mention but a few.

If you can get a large advance from a publisher then you are certainly going to increase the probability that the publisher will really do something with your book but that isn't essential. Every year many books become major bestsellers that have had advances of as little as $5,000.

9. Why can't I find my book in the bookstore?

That is the $64,000 question and the one that probably drives most authors crazy.

There are 30,000 reasons for that problem because there are approximately 30,000 hardcover books published every year. Most bookstores order only two or three copies of a book and, in some cases, a store may not order a book at all (except for the big book chains like Dalton and Waldenbooks). It is impossible for every bookstore to have every book in stock.

Unfortunately, there is not much that you can do to remedy the situation aside from hope that your publisher will print sufficient copies of the book and get behind it.

Alas, most of the 30,000 books that are published are dead before they are published and probably shouldn't have been published at all. If a book is going to have a printing of only 2,000 copies (and many books do), then it has been a waste of everybody's time and money.

10. **Are some publishers better than others?**

You bet, they are. There are marked differences among publishers especially when it comes to certain kinds of books. There are publishers that know how to handle fiction better than others, publishers that are better with cookbooks, publishers that understand what to do with a physical fitness book, and there are publishers that are better at promotion and advertising and, of course, publishers that have better sales organizations than others.

How to select the right publisher for your book is one of the tricks of the trade and an excellent reason for using an agent who should know the strengths and weaknesses of most publishers.

Most authors, however, don't have the opportunity of selecting the right publisher because unless their book property is in demand by more than one publisher, they will probably have to accept the first publisher who makes an offer. That is the reality of the situation.

11. **How important is your editor in the success of your book?**

The editor is everything. Not only is the editor the one who is ultimately responsible for the quality of the manuscript but it is the editor who creates the excitement within the publishing firm and with the sales force for the book.

It is usually the editor who writes the catalog copy for the book and if the editor is able to convince the publisher that the book is worth a full page in the catalog, that will help to launch the book better than if a book is relegated to a half page or even a quarter page in the catalog.

Editors usually write flapcopy for the book and work with the art department on jacket designs.

It is also the editor who usually presents the book at the semiannual sales conferences. I have attended many sales conferences where a first-rate book was given a second-rate presentation by the editor, and the sales potential for the book suffered as a result. Conversely, a book often doesn't measure up to the sales presentation made by the editor.

An editor's credibility with the sales organization is also important. If the editor is one who has brought the publishing firm big bestsellers in the past, then the salespeople are more likely to believe that editor when he presents a book and says it will sell well.

The bottom line really is that in many instances the editor is as important as the company.

12. **How can I get on the "Donahue" program to talk about my book?**

It is true that an appearance on "Donahue" can have a very positive effect on the sales of a book but it is equally true that the Donahue staff is very selective about whom they invite to appear on the program. Guests on the "Donahue" program have to appear for an hour, so not only does the subject matter have to be strong and have appeal for the Donahue audience but the author has to be articulate or at least be able to answer questions clearly.

Every day publishers present dozens of books to the Donahue staff and the competition is tough. Even if you were Phil Donahue's best friend, I doubt if Phil would have you on the program if he didn't believe you would be the right guest. Above all, Donahue and his producers understand their audience and they won't compromise for any author.

13. **What kind of books are publishers looking for?**

I guess the simplest answer to that question is books that sell. Most publishers don't limit themselves to any particular kind of book but rather to books that will not only sell but will fit into their publishing list.

Often I have submitted a book on a particular subject to a publisher and had the book turned down because the publisher already had a book on that subject on their current publishing list.

I also have had publishers call me and say, "We're looking for a good book on buying a home," or "Are you representing any books about Ronald Reagan?"

Publishers always have holes in their list of books and may be on the lookout for a celebrity book or a novel set in the West or a fine biography of an American hero. It all depends on the house, what they are currently publishing, and what kind of books are under contract.

14. What should I do if I am writing a book and have a contract and then discover that another writer is doing a book on the same subject for another publisher?

I think I can best answer the question with a publishing story from my own experience.

A number of years ago a doctor by the name of William Sweeney and his co-author, Barbara Lang Stern, were writing a book for William Morrow titled *A Woman's Doctor,* which I represented. Halfway through the writing of the book, we learned that Doubleday had a book by the title of *A Woman's Doctor* under contract.

We were concerned because it didn't seem to any of us that there was a need or, for that matter, a market for both books.

The concern proved to be unnecessary. Although both books were published within a short time of each other, our book was much more successful and was, as a matter of fact, one of the most successful books I have ever developed. Our book was a Reader's Digest Condensed Book Club selection and had a healthy hardcover sale and a very solid paperback sale.

Why did *A Woman's Doctor* by Sweeney and Stern make it despite the competition?

It had a lot to do with the fact that Dr. Sweeney was a very promotable author and, perhaps even more important, William Morrow really got behind our book, obviously determined to make the book work despite the presence of the Doubleday book.

If you are writing a book and another author is doing exactly the same subject, don't abandon your project unless there are unusual or extenuating circumstances.

15. How can I stop somebody from stealing my book idea?

You can't do much about someone who steals your book idea, but if you remember that you can't publish an idea, you won't be so concerned.

An idea is only as good as the execution and if someone else is going to write a book based on your idea, he is going to have to do a lot of work—and do it well.

I don't recall hearing about many book ideas being "stolen" in book publishing and ideas are loosely and freely and frequently discussed by editors, agents and writers without much worry.

Somebody still has to write the book.

16. Isn't it better to have your book published in hardcover before paperback?

That is one of the primary misconceptions about book publishing.

There are decided advantages for certain books to be published in hardcover first but because of the high cost of producing books, more and more books are published in either trade paperback or mass market paperback.

A trade paperback is usually priced higher than a mass market paperback and lower than a hardcover book.

In the summer of 1981, I represented a book that, although published in hardcover, was simultaneously distributed in greater quantities as a trade paperback. The book was *Pills That Don't Work* by Dr. Sidney M. Wolfe, Christopher M. Coley and the Health Research Group founded by Ralph Nader. The hardcover edition was priced at $15.00 and the trade paperback edition at $6.95.

The trade paperback edition became number four on the *New York Times* Trade Paperback Best Sellers list.

If *Pills That Don't Work* had been published primarily as a hardcover book, I am doubtful that we would have sold that many copies. It was a book that definitely should have been published as a trade paperback.

There are many books that should never be published in hardcover and are mass market paperback properties only. Many authors have had enormous financial success without ever having had their books published in hardcover. Of course, for many writers, it is more prestigious to have their books published in hardcover and it does increase your chances of being reviewed.

It is best to give some thought to whether your book belongs in hardcover at all, but in the end your publisher will make that determination for you.

17. Do you have to be a really good writer to write a book?

It helps, but the truth is that today the quality of the writing does not seem to play the same role that it did twenty years ago.

You still have to know how to write an English sentence and the way that you express yourself is important, but beyond that you can succeed and be published if you have a strong idea or are an expert in a particular field.

The best word to describe books that seem to make it these days is "readable." If the book tells a good story or presents thoughts that appeal to others, then you have a chance.

Execution and readability are what really count.

18. Should I publish my book myself if I can't get a publisher?

If you believe strongly in your book and aren't just on an ego trip and if you have the money to gamble, then why not? But I certainly would advise you not to try to publish your own book if you have a publisher who is willing to do it for you.

I have often been asked, "With all the good ideas for books that you have had, haven't you ever had the urge to publish a book yourself?"

My answer is: "Whenever I get that urge, I lie down until it passes."

There just aren't any guarantees in publishing a book and in many ways publishing is like the movie business or Broadway—it's a big gamble.

If you are determined to publish your own book, either because you can't find a publisher or because you believe that no publisher can do the right job for you, proceed with caution.

First, stay away from the so-called "vanity" book publishers such as Exposition Press, Vantage, Comet, Pageant Press and William Frederick. These publishers offer to publish virtually any book for a substantial fee. The vanity book publishers rarely get books into bookstores and their promotion usually consists of very limited advertising.

If you really want to publish your own book, then you will have to find an established publisher or book distribution organization like Caroline House. There are publishers who will distribute a book for an independent publisher (you) but they still aren't that easy to find. In order for a publisher to want to take on the distribution of your book, he not only has to be convinced that the book has a chance to sell but that you will get behind the book with advertising and promotion.

Recently, I represented a book by Al and Alice Howard titled *Turn Your Kitchen into a Gold Mine*. I was able to get offers for the book from Rawson, Wade and Crown but Al Howard wasn't satisfied and decided to publish the book himself. He formed a corporation and was able to arrange for Harper & Row to distribute the book.

Al Howard is a former advertising man and he advertised his book well. *Turn Your Kitchen into a Gold Mine* has sold over 70,000 copies at $12.95 and was number five on the *Time* magazine Best Seller list.

Now Al Howard is negotiating for the paperback rights for his book which he owns 100%, and since he and his wife are not only the authors but the publishers, they don't have to split the revenues from the paperback rights with the hardcover publisher.

Pat Wright had even greater success when he published *On a Clear*

Day You Can See General Motors himself which was distributed by Caroline House.

So it can be done, but the odds are still against your success and if you have the chance to be published by a legitimate publisher, grab it.

19. If I don't meet the deadline for my book, will the publisher cancel my contract?

When you sign a contract for a book you and the publisher agree to a specific date on which the finished and acceptable manuscript will be completed. Many publishers' contracts have a thirty- to ninety-day grace period after the agreed upon delivery date in the contract, but in fact the publisher has the legal right to cancel the contract and, in most cases, ask for the return of payments made to the author.

That is the legal situation but in reality it doesn't work that way.

Most publishers understand that it isn't always possible to finish a manuscript on exactly the date agreed on in a contract since no one can predict exactly how long it will take to write a book.

It is always a wise move to keep your editor informed if you are going to be late with your manuscript. If you are a few weeks or even a few months late, most publishers will understand as long as timelines or some other factor doesn't make meeting the delivery date essential.

Since the delivery date for a manuscript is part of the contract and therefore legally binding, it is smart to give yourself as much time as possible when you agree on a date. It's better to have a realistic date when you sign the contract than to have problems later.

I have represented authors whose books have been two, three and even four years late. Why are publishers willing to wait that long?

Usually it is because the author is either very well known or the book involves a celebrity and the publisher will be happy whenever he gets the book.

Publishers are often willing to give authors a long time to deliver a book if it is a subject that requires a lot of research and travel or if the author just happens to be a slow writer.

The average time for an author to deliver an acceptable book is generally nine months to a year.

20. What makes a manuscript acceptable to a publisher?

It's a subjective decision usually made by the editor or, if there is a dispute, by the editor-in-chief or the president of the publishing firm.

Acceptable manuscripts mean just that. Acceptable in the opinion of the publisher—not the author.

There are a very few authors who don't have an acceptance clause in their contracts. What they turn in to the publisher, the publisher must publish.

There are publishers who will negotiate a "first proceeds" clause into a contract which means that if the publisher finds your manuscript unacceptable you will have to pay back the advance you have received only if you find another publisher. You then pay from the first proceeds from your new publisher.

19

Uncle Bill's Helpful Publishing Hints

THIS chapter is not to be confused with *Mary Ellen's Best of Helpful Hints* but, in a way, I hope to accomplish the same thing—not around the house—but around the book business. These are my helpful publishing hints for authors, would-be authors, editors, publishers, agents or anyone who has more than a passing interest in book publishing.

- Advertise in the *New York Times* on Saturday on the book page. The rates are cheaper and since few publishers advertise on a Saturday you have a shot at getting more attention.

- If your publisher tells you he is going to publish your book in time for the Christmas season, make sure he ships the books before Thanksgiving. Otherwise tell him to wait until after the first of the year. After Thanksgiving, the stores hardly have time to open the cartons.

- Did you know Howard Cosell has a network radio program over ABC called "Speaking of Everything" which is a great place to promote a book? It is on every Sunday evening from ten to ten-thirty and Howard is always looking for interesting, stimulating guests.

◆ If you call Mike Wallace at CBS with a book that will make a good, strong segment for him on "60 Minutes," chances are you will be able to get to him. But don't bother to write or call Wallace if the story has already been all over the place. Mike insists on the story first.

◆ The new, hot book interview program is Charlie Rose's telecast out of WRC-TV in Washington, D.C. Rose is now in thirty-two cities and on the lookout for good guests.

◆ Job security in book publishing isn't what it used to be. If you are going into book publishing as a career, save your money as you go along.

◆ *The Village Voice* "ain't what it used to be." Don't knock yourself out to publicize your book in the *Voice*.

◆ If you want to sell a sports book, try Victor Temkin at Berkley.

◆ Farrar, Straus & Giroux may be the classiest publisher in the business.

◆ Myrna Blyth, the new, determined editor-in-chief at *Ladies' Home Journal*, has the fastest checkbook in town. She is spending big to help the *Journal* recapture its old glory.

◆ Dick Kaplan, the pleasant, talented editor-in-chief at *US* magazine is on the lookout for book properties. I would go to Kaplan if *People* turns you down.

◆ If you have a celebrity book to sell, try Ellis Amburn at Putnam's. Ellis and celebrities go hand in hand. Among others, Ellis edited Shelley Winters's book when he was at William Morrow.

◆ The most reliable, dependable, conscientious editor in book publishing is Howard Cady at William Morrow.

◆ Richard Marek, who now has his own imprint affiliated with St. Martin's Press, is a good mark for a commercial first novel. It was Marek, when he was affiliated with Putnam's, who built Robert Ludlum. Not bad!

- Cat books will always sell!

- Evan Thomas at W. W. Norton is one of the true gentlemen in book publishing. He is courteous, returns phone calls and will spend time with you and your author even if he doesn't buy your book.

- Don't submit an outline for a book to a publisher with fifteen title suggestions. Go with one. Fifteen titles (or even two) indicate someone who can't make up his mind.

- The women in book publishing are much more aggressive than the men. If you want someone to really push your book, try a female editor.

- Beautiful art or picture books belong at Harry Abrams.

- Get to know the sales director at the publishing firm. He is the one who can really help (or hurt) the book.

- The best bookstore in New York is Scribner's on Fifth Avenue. It has old-world charm.

- Larry Ashmead at Harper & Row is a very productive editor. He likes lots of product.

- If your book is excerpted in *Book Digest*, don't get too excited. They don't pay a lot of money and can't really affect the sale of a book.

- John Mack Carter is the dean of the magazine editors. John runs (and very well) *Good Housekeeping*. If you want to sell a book excerpt to *Good Housekeeping*, the man to contact is Len Dowty.

- If you really want to impress people in book publishing, open a house account at the Four Seasons restaurant.

- The movie people can drive you crazy asking for manuscripts or galleys for books. Ninety-nine times out of a hundred, they never buy—not even an option.

- Don't submit your book proposal on colored paper to attract attention. Plain white (8½ x 11) is perfect.

- Publishers often have sheep mentality. If a book about pills sells big, then thirty-three publishers will be looking for a book about pills.

- Typographical errors and bad spelling are "no-nos" for a book proposal.

- Try to find an agent with a sense of humor. You will both need it. Sterling Lord has a sense of humor.

- Books for retired people have a very limited market. Most retired people can't afford to buy books.

- Publishers aren't necessarily impressed by people with beards. You don't have to grow one to look like a real writer.

- Books that win awards don't necessarily sell.

- Peter Schwed at Simon & Schuster is one of the best editors for sports books.

- There are some good agents who specialize in juvenile books. Some of them are Marilyn Marlow at Curtis Brown, Dorothy Markinko at McIntosh & Otis, Betty Marks, Jean V. Naggar, and Amy Berkower at Writers House.

- One of the best editors of cookbooks is Judith Jones at Knopf.

- Discover something new about Hitler and World War II and you have the start of a book.

- There are some editors who don't return phone calls and that's a bad habit. They know who they are.

- Don't have a few drinks at lunch before you go to meet with your editor, agent or publisher even if you are nervous.

- An author who is a pain in the neck because he or she is continually calling on the phone will quickly wear out his welcome. Unless the author is a big seller, many editors would rather not do business with writers who drive them crazy.

- Don't arrive unannounced at your editor's office. You especially shouldn't try it at Simon & Schuster because they have a guard at the elevators.

- When you are negotiating your contract, try to get the publisher to pay for the index. Indexing can be expensive.

- If you want an attorney in New York who won't take forever in going over your book contract, try Egon Dumler at Dumler & Giroux at 575 Madison Avenue.

- More people are suing for libel and plagiarism than ever before. Be careful.

- One of the best foreign markets for your book is Japan. One of the best Japanese agents is Tom Mori of the Tuttle-Mori Agency.

- Publishers are more litigious than ever. If you don't deliver your book, they are likely to sue. The most aggressive publisher in going after authors for money owed is Simon & Schuster.

- Grosset & Dunlap is one of the slowest payers in book publishing.

- Paul Stuart on Madison Avenue is where the well dressed male editors buy their clothes.

- Never trust the opinion of an editor under twenty-five.

- Don't spend the first half of your publisher's advance until the book is finished and you have received the second half of the advance. The first half is *only* a loan until they decide to publish the *finished* manuscript.

- Rob Fitz at Macmillan is a pleasant, outgoing, young editor who is easy to deal with.

- Regional books can sell well and Doubleday is the best publisher for regional books.

- Ferris Mack at Doubleday, who has been there forever, is easy to get to and has one of the best senses of humor in the business. Very little upsets Ferris Mack.

- If you want to sell a book on a Jewish subject, it is best to try a non-Jewish editor. They think Jewish books sell big.

- If a bookstore asks you to autograph books for them to sell, do it. Autographed books cannot be returned to the publisher.

- Most publishers give you ten free copies of your book and will let you buy additional copies at a discount.

- Have your friends buy your book—don't give them copies. It will help sales at the retail level.

- Hollywood agents are not to be trusted.

- Anthologies are better off not being published.

- Scribner's pays very small advances but they are a quality publisher.

- Doubleday is not the best place for an editor if you want to make a lot of money.

- Simon & Schuster is the best place for an editor to make a lot of money, especially if they hire you away from another publishing firm. There are more senior editors making more money at Simon & Schuster than any other publishing firm.

- The best book idea person is Bill Adler. The second best is Bill Adler.

- The odds in favor of your hardcover book being sold to a paperback publisher are fair to poor.

- The prettiest woman in book publishing is Susan Kamil, the vice president for subsidiary rights at Simon & Schuster.

- Don't call your editor or publisher at home unless it is a real, real emergency. It's probably not an emergency and can wait until morning.

- Likewise your agent.

- The best American agent in London is Abner Stein. He is an American who lives in London and knows all the British publishers (and they like him).

- Check your book galleys carefully. Typos and mistakes are not uncommon.

- *Cosmopolitan* magazine pays very little for book rights and they usually buy only second serial.

- *Playboy* is one of the best markets for first serial rights for books that appeal to men.

- Isaac Asimov may be the most prolific writer in publishing history.

- Publishing is a business that thrives on gossip.

- The competition among the "Big Five" in the women's magazines for first serial rights to hot books is fierce. The Big Five are *Ladies' Home Journal, Good Housekeeping, McCalls, Woman's Day* and *Family Circle.*

- If you could convince Bill Moyers to write a book about Lyndon Johnson and you were his agent or publisher, you could make a lot of money.

- Timing is everything in book publishing: The *right* book at the *right* time with the *right* publisher.

- Not enough editors, agents and authors spend enough time in bookstores. They have no idea what is happening on the retail level.

- Don't have too many friends, relatives or loved ones read your manuscript before you submit it to your editor. They will only confuse or upset you—or even give you false hope.

- Don't write a book about the television business; they don't sell. That goes for books about Broadway too.

- Roger Donald at Little, Brown is a first-rate editor. He cares.

- I once had some dealings with Aaron Priest, the agent who represents, among others, Erma Bombeck, and once was enough.

- You don't have to copyright your manuscript. The publisher does that when the book is published.

- An unusual but good publisher to place an "informational" book with is Facts On File. Ed Knappman is the executive editor.

- If you are going to write fiction, read fiction, especially fiction that sells.

- Times Books may be part of the *New York Times* but they haven't made it yet as a book publisher. Perhaps their new editor-in-chief, Jonathan Segal, will change that.

- If you are a man and your editor is a woman (or vice versa), don't make a pass at her. It won't help.

- If you have a book to sell, you are often better off with a small publisher. Sometimes the big publishers have too full a plate.

- When an editor tells you "tomorrow," he really doesn't mean it.

- Next to Swifty Lazar, agent Robbie Lantz may represent more Hollywood and Broadway stars than anybody.

- Simon & Schuster may have the best copy editing department in book publishing—and copy editing is important.

- A good copy editor can help put a book that murders the English language into acceptable shape.

- If you bring or introduce a book property to an agent, ask for a piece of the action. No one should do anything for nothing.

- If you are going to have a cocktail party to launch your book, don't waste too much money. Cocktail parties hardly ever sell books.

- Editors take authors and agents out to lunch and dinner. An editor without a liberal expense account has a problem.

- A thirteen-year-old kid now has a book on the trade paperback bestseller list. His name is Patrick Bossert and the title of his book is *You Can Do the Cube*. So there's hope for you.

- Harper & Row has the most frustrating telephone service in the business. You can wait for a long time before they answer.

- Publishing is a business of first names. You don't have to be formal.

- If you are sending around a book proposal, don't date it. The editor who sees an "old" date on a proposal may think it has been around.

- Only superagents and superauthors really get rich in book publishing.

How to Promote a Book

THE best place to promote a book in the eighties is on television and the best place to promote a book on television is the "Donahue" program.

"Donahue," which is now seen in 218 cities, has in a way revolutionized the promotion of books. If you are lucky enough to have your book introduced on "Donahue" you have a real chance to sell a lot of copies. More bestsellers have been made as a result of an appearance on "Donahue" than on any other program in television history.

There are two simple reasons for this phenomenon. One is that Donahue gives a book one hour of time, not four minutes or thirty seconds as is frequently the case on other programs. Phil really gets into the guts of the book and doesn't just hold up the jacket. If an author is on the Donahue program he gets a good opportunity to really discuss his book and present it to the audience.

The second reason is the composition of the Donahue audience. At least 80 percent of Phil's audience consists of women, and women are the major buyers of books in this country.

Another reason that "Donahue" works so well for books is that the women in the audience have a chance to ask the author questions and probe into the content of the book. The program is intelligent and the quality of the audience and the guests is first-rate.

I would prefer to have an author I represent appear on the "Donahue" program than have a full-page ad in the *New York Times Book Review* four weeks in a row.

Other television programs that can contribute to the success of a book are the "Today" show, "Good Morning America," "Merv Griffin" and the "Tonight" show. The only drawback to appearing on "Good Morning America" or "Today" is how little time the author is given to discuss the book.

Bryant Gumbel, Jane Pauley, David Hartman and Joan Lunden do intelligent interviews and they usually do their homework. There have been instances when an appearance on "Today" or "Good Morning America" has had a positive effect on the sale of a book.

The "Today" show and "Good Morning America" are, I think, equal in their impact on book sales. The competition between the two programs is fierce and if you are asked to appear on one to discuss your book, your chances of appearing on the other are virtually nil.

Both programs have staffs that not only research books but preinterview the guests to make sure that they are articulate enough to be interesting interviewees on television.

Merv Griffin has made a lot of bestsellers as a result of an author appearing on his program.

The most recent example I can think of is *The Beverly Hills Diet*. Judy Mazel made an initial appearance on the Merv Griffin program and that was the catalyst for the remarkable success of the book.

Griffin gives sufficient time to authors appearing on his program—in some cases ten to fifteen minutes—and although it is not the same amount of time that an author can receive on the "Donahue" program, it certainly is sufficient.

Merv Griffin is also very considerate of the authors who appear on his program and will always hold up the jacket of the book at least once or twice so that the author gets the best shot at promoting his book.

Griffin is not afraid of controversial books and he selects authors who will appeal to the people who watch his program.

It used to be that appearances on the "Tonight" show when Jack Paar was the host were reflected immediately by increased sales. Jack Paar made a lot of bestsellers including his own book, *Three on a Toothbrush*.

Johnny Carson, when he first took over the "Tonight" show, also devoted considerable time to books but of late that doesn't seem to be the case. Carson has a few authors who appear on his program frequently like Carl Sagan and certainly Sagan's appearances on the Carson show have contributed to the success of his books.

It is not true that exposure on television will guarantee increased sales. Sometimes an appearance can have a negative effect on the sales of the book if the author does not present the book well. Obviously, an articulate and attractive author who can present his book in an interesting manner is as important in many cases as a well-written manuscript.

There are a number of other television programs around the country that can help the sale of a book. They include the Bob Braun program in Cincinnati, the Charlie Rose program in Washington, D.C. (both of these programs appear in a number of cities) and, of course, the Mike Douglas show and the new, syndicated television program, "The Hour."

Virtually every major city in the country has local programs that are helpful to the promotion of a book. In Washington it is "Panorama"; in New York it is "Live At Five," "Joe Franklin" and Bill Boggs's "Midday"; in Chicago it is "A. M. Chicago" and "Chicago Today"; in San Francisco, "People Are Talking" and "A. M. San Francisco"; "Good Morning Boston"; "A. M. Philadelphia"; "Kelley & Company" in Detroit; and "Hour Magazine" in Los Angeles.

Radio interviews can be helpful to the success of a book but the impact is not as strong as television. There are, however, some programs that can positively affect the sale of the book. One is the "Larry King Show" which is heard every night from midnight to five-thirty on the entire Mutual network in more than 200 cities nationwide. Larry King has a large and faithful audience.

Although King admits that he never reads a book before the author appears on the program, he is a fabulous interviewer and if an author is lucky enough to appear on the "Larry King Show," it certainly will be a big plus for his book. Larry will frequently have the author on for the entire program, and the author will answer phone calls from listeners around the country.

There are a number of local radio programs on which authors are interviewed that also have an impact on the market. They include Barry Farber in New York, Michael Jackson in California, Frank Harden and Jack Weaver in Washington, D. C., Bill Calder in New Orleans, Rex Ryan in Grand Rapids, Shelly Tromberg in Washington, D. C. and Dave Andrews in Fall River, Massachusetts.

There have been occasions when "60 Minutes" on CBS or "20/20" on ABC or the NBC "Magazine" program have conducted in-depth interviews with an author when a book is published. If that should happen it can be as big or as positive in terms of sales as an appearance on the "Donahue" program.

"60 Minutes" reaches an audience of forty to fifty million viewers every week whereas "Donahue" reaches an audience of eight million each day. By virtue of sheer numbers "60 Minutes" is way out in front.

Right after the "Donahue" program and the other major television programs, the second most important factor in the promotion of a book is a book-signing where an author has the drawing power to attract two to three hundred customers to a bookstore to purchase a book. It is a great way to start the book off to becoming a bestseller. It is especially helpful if the store at which the author is signing books is one that reports each week to the *New York Times* Best Sellers list.

The names of stores that report to the *New York Times* Best Sellers list are supposed to be a secret, but publishers know most of the names and it is not difficult to set up book-signings at those stores.

When I was involved with Howard Cosell's first book, *Cosell by Cosell,* the book was launched by a book-signing at Kroch's & Brentano's in Chicago, which may be the largest bookstore in America. I knew he had a hit the minute the book-signing began. The lines inside and outside the store were enormous. We must have sold at least 400 books in the space of two or three hours.

Since Kroch's & Brentano's is one of the stores that reports to the *New York Times* Best Sellers list, it was a great beginning for Cosell's book which quickly became a national bestseller and was on the *Times* list for more than six months.

Generating activity in bookstores through book-signings can really promote sales, and I believe very strongly in using that technique whenever the opportunity presents itself.

Much has been written—and a lot of it negative—about author tours. Authors frequently complain, with some justification, that when they go out to promote their books in a particular city, their books aren't even in the stores or, if they are, distribution is very poor.

This, of course, does not occur with the major book properties, but it is certainly true that an author can go to a city to make appearances on radio and television and to give newspaper interviews about his book and yet the book is not really available in that city.

No one has ever been able to lick this problem and therefore it is always wise to contact the sales department at the publishing firm to make sure that books are available and adequately displayed in stores in the cities where the author is touring and promoting.

Many of the major book publishers are involved in the promotion of too many books at the same time and therefore they cannot give proper attention to each of the books they are promoting. The big books get most of the attention and the other authors have to pray that they will find their books in stores and be able to get adequate promotion on radio and television and in the newspapers.

It is also important for an author to be briefed on how he should present and discuss his book in the media. It doesn't make sense for an author who has written a book called *How to Stay Thin* to spend all of his time on radio or television or in newspaper interviews discussing his wonderful grandmother in Iowa who has celebrated her hundredth birthday.

I have advised authors I have represented to be sure that the conversation with the interviewer does not wander too far from the book subject. They must get the conversation back to the book, otherwise the interview will be a waste of time.

21

The Gospel According to Adler

- Publishers are nice people but in the final analysis they are only concerned with the bottom line—profit and loss.
- Never discuss a book idea with an editor at the end of the day or when he or she is preparing for a sales conference.
- Whenever possible, deal with an editor who has influence.
- If you have a "hot" property, try to have a "hot" agent represent you. They have more muscle.
- Don't always hold out for the top price for your book. I have seen book deals quickly evaporate. Be a closer, not a haggler.
- Don't give up. Last week we sold a book to a publisher after it had been turned down by forty-two other publishers.
- Stay away from lawyers. Chances are they will get you nothing but legal bills.
- Don't offer your book property just to the major publishers. That's what everybody does.
- Don't quit your job the day you sign a contract for your first novel.
- You are not writing the Bible. Listen to a smart editor and make changes.

- If you are going to be a writer, write every day—even on weekends and your birthday. It's like playing the violin. You have to practice and practice.
- Don't try to write the great American novel your first time out. Just a good, publishable story would be fine.
- Try to meet your deadlines.
- Avoid tough option clauses in book contracts. They can haunt you later on.
- Don't expect publishers to pay royalties exactly on the day they are due.
- Use an agent. You are better off with one than without one.
- When you are published be prepared for the shock of not finding your book in every bookstore.
- Try to have your book published by a house that has its own sales force rather than by a publisher that distributes its books through another company's sales force.
- Visit bookstores. You can't write books unless you know what other people are writing.
- Don't send a Christmas gift to your editor. It won't help.
- The first rule for success in book publishing is that the best person to promote your book is you. Don't count on the publisher to do it for you.
- If you think that dedicating your book to your editor will help—guess again. You are better off dedicating the book to your mother. She will really appreciate it.
- Don't try to write another *Beverly Hills Diet.* It's already been written.
- Book publishers have a short attention span. If your book doesn't sell quickly, they will soon forget you and your book.
- Consider writing a paperback original. There can be a lot of money in originals.
- Try to publish with a firm where the editors don't come and go in rapid succession.
- Every book doesn't have to be edited by Michael Korda. There are a lot of other good editors in town.
- Don't write another book analyzing Richard Nixon. They don't sell.

- If your publisher promises you a full-page ad in the *New York Times*, get it in writing.
- You may think you can write as funny as Erma Bombeck, but you can't.
- The chances of your book being made into a motion picture are about as good as your chances of becoming the president of the United States.
- Having lunch or dinner with your editor won't gain you much more than a few calories.
- Don't expect your editor to read your 400-page manuscript overnight.
- Everyone who wrote for his school newspaper will not necessarily write the great American novel.
- When your book is published, don't give away copies to your friends. Have them buy their own copies. It will help your sales.
- Remember an advance is really just a loan. If you don't deliver a satisfactory manuscript, the publisher will want the advance back.
- Everyone who is a great cook shouldn't write a cookbook.
- Sex books are not big—even if it is a book about *your* sex life. Forget it.
- Your favorite subject is not necessarily the best subject for a book. Not everyone has the same burning desire to know all there is to know about the blue-tipped butterflies of Argentina.
- Don't publish with a "vanity" publisher. Your vanity won't really be satisfied and you will have lost a considerable amount of money.
- Every book doesn't have to be published in time for the Christmas season. People buy books the other eleven months of the year too.
- When you are interviewed by a talk show host, don't expect the host to have read your book.
- Children's books are much harder to write than you think—and even more difficult to get published.
- Doubleday publishes too many books every year and if you publish with them, your book may get lost.

- There is nothing wrong with having your book excerpted in the *National Enquirer*. More people read the *Enquirer* than any other paper in America.
- Over 30,000 books are published every year and the *New York Times* can't review them all.
- Self-help books can sell well but there are too many of them.
- Don't expect your editor to rewrite your book for you.
- The most important department at a good publishing house is copy editing.
- Simon & Schuster has always done the best advertising in the business and that's because Strome Lamon is the best ad director in book publishing.
- Arbor House runs a close second when it comes to advertising. Their budgets may be smaller but their imagination is first-rate.
- Lyle Stuart is the most controversial man in book publishing.
- The glory days for reprint sales are probably over.
- The role of an agent in the success of a book is usually overrated.
- Your chances of making a living as a full-time writer are as good as your chances of playing first base for the New York Yankees.
- Sports books don't sell. Neither do books about life after death.
- Most author's talents are not equal to their egos.
- James Michener is probably the most successful writer in America.
- Gladys Carr, the editor-in-chief of McGraw-Hill trade books, may be one of the smartest editors in the business.
- If Hugh Hefner would write his autobiography, it would be a big bestseller.
- By 1985 all the literary agents will be charging a commission of 15%.
- Jimmy Carter's memoirs won't sell and neither will Jody Powell's.
- William Safire is the best book property in Washington, D.C.
- Charles Rembar is the best known attorney in book publishing.
- Books about composers have a small market.
- Don't knock Judith Krantz. She sells.
- The best editor for fiction is Phyllis Grann at G. P. Putnam's.

- The best publisher for diet books is Rawson Associates.
- The best overall publisher is William Morrow.
- Conglomerates have saved book publishing. Without them, few publishers could afford to publish.
- You can't write fiction unless you read fiction.
- If you get an agent for your book, don't call him or her every day. When there is news, you will be the first to know.
- Irving Mansfield probably knows more about promoting books than anyone else.
- Don't expect your publisher to publish your finished manuscript overnight. Allow at least six months.
- If your publisher invites you to present your book at the sales conference, do it!
- Most editors are not particularly good idea people.
- Most editors are not very good business people.
- Random House gives its senior editors more autonomy than other publishers.
- Publishers are taking longer to pay their bills.
- Writing is the loneliest job in the world.
- Rosalyn Carter's book will sell better than Jimmy's.
- When Greta Garbo dies, there will be at least six books about the "real" Garbo.
- Frank Sinatra will sue you if you write a book about him that he doesn't like.
- Philip Spitzer is the nicest agent in the business.
- Editors would be in big trouble if they were responsible for profit and loss.
- Irv Goodman at Viking is the nicest publisher in the business.
- Peter Schwed at Simon & Schuster is remarkable. He has more energy and vitality than editors twenty years his junior.
- Financial books aren't so big any more—no one can afford to buy them.
- The Book-of-the-Month Club is more prestigious than the Literary Guild.

- In five years, Simon & Schuster will be the General Motors of book publishing.
- One of the questions I'm asked most frequently is, "Can I use a book title if it has been used before?" Titles can't be copyrighted but you certainly couldn't write a book called *The Beverly Hills Diet* since the courts would consider that unfair competition.
- If, however, a title was used a number of years ago, there is no reason why it can't be used again unless the first book was an enormous bestseller. This is especially true if the original book is out of print.
- There should be more regional book publishers so that the books that are published can better reflect the *entire* country.
- It seems as if there are more psychiatrists and physicians writing books than there are practicing medicine. No wonder doctors don't have time for house calls—they are all busy dictating their manuscripts.
- Authors should pay more attention to the catalog copy written by editors for their books. Catalog copy is very important since in most instances it is the publisher's catalog that the sales force carries into the bookstores. Ask your editor to let you see the catalog copy before it is finalized.
- Unless photographs are absolutely essential to a book, I would vote against including photographs in most books since they add so significantly to the production cost of a book.
- Too many books have jacket designs that are unimaginative and unappealing. The jacket is supposed to sell a book, not kill a possible sale. A smart author will ask to see the jacket design before it goes into production.
- Most royalty statements are impossible to figure out and even after all these years, I still struggle to make heads or tails out of some of the royalty statements from major publishers.

  If you don't understand a royalty statement, don't be shy, ask the publisher to explain it.
- I have always thought the book industry should try to convince one of the television networks to do for book publishing what has been done for motion pictures, television and the theater—namely, an awards program like the Oscars, the Emmys and the Tonys.

A glamorous program could be put together that would have a wide audience because so many celebrities are writing books and could appear on the program to encourage the public to buy more books, which obviously would be helpful to us all.

- More books are written by people on the East Coast on a per capita basis than any other place in the country but more best-sellers are written by authors on the West Coast.

- One of the best foreign markets for American books is the Japanese market. They have a voracious appetite for American literature, especially in the self-help area.

- Humor sells; satire very rarely does.

- There are more and more freelance publicists helping publishers and authors to promote books. A freelance publicist can be of great assistance because the publicist who works independently can aggressively promote your book. Freelance publicists are usually engaged by the publisher but on occasion an author will hire a freelance publicist. The best directory of publicists who work in the book field can be found in the *LMP* published by Bowker.

  If I were an author who was concerned about the kind of publicity job the publisher was going to do, I would seriously explore the possibility of hiring a freelance publicist. They can make the difference.

- Some very good publishing is being done by the university presses around the country, but I can never understand why the major presses don't get together for joint promotion and merchandising of their books.

  The only problem with being published by a university press is that your chances for adequate distribution in bookstores or for promotion or publicity are not all that good. Occasionally, however, a university press book will break out and sell very well.

- There are many book awards but the only ones that really increase the sale of a book are the Nobel Prize and the Pulitzer Prize.

- Perhaps the first woman to make her mark in book publishing was Helen Meyer of Dell Publishing. Before she retired and before Dell was sold to Doubleday, Helen Meyer ran that company with an iron hand. Long before Women's Lib was fashionable and before women began to have the impact in book publishing that they have today, Helen Meyer was in the forefront of the industry.

◆ I can never understand why editors talk to authors about a possible new book without first mentioning the possibility to the author's agent. Frequently, after I have brought an author to a particular publisher, the editor will discuss a book idea with the author without even having the courtesy or good judgment to notify me.

It is only when the authors mention their conversations with the editors that I am aware that the meetings have taken place. It obviously makes the agent feel as if he were out in the cold, and I don't think it is a wise move for the publisher to talk with the author without first running it by the agent.

◆ Anyone who writes a book and doesn't expect aggravation should forget about writing the book.

◆ One of the last of the independent publishers, Dodd, Mead, was recently bought by Thomas Nelson, a successful publisher of religious books. That brings the number of independent publishers still profitably functioning down to a very few.

The major independent publishers who don't have to report to another company include Crown, Farrar, Straus, M. Evans and W. W. Norton.

◆ Most publishers know very little about direct mail advertising or how to promote a book with advertising that is designed to pull in immediate sales with coupons. However, two of the best publishers in this area over the years have been Simon & Schuster and Random House.

More publishers should develop the talent for direct mail advertising. It is an important avenue for selling books and one that most publishers have not even touched in terms of its potential.

◆ John Mack Carter and Bob Stein are two of the most remarkable senior magazine editors in this country.

John Mack Carter runs *Good Housekeeping* and Bob Stein is the editor-in-chief of *McCalls*. Between them they have edited more magazine articles and more book condensations and have written more lines of copy for magazine covers than any two editors in the country.

John Mack Carter is unique in the business because he is the only magazine editor to have been editor-in-chief of three major women's magazines—*McCalls, Ladies' Home Journal* and, now, *Good Housekeeping.*

Both Stein and Carter are creative and pleasant individuals who deserve all the success they have had. The same can be said for their counterparts at *Women's Day* (Geraldine Rhoads) and *Family Circle* (Arthur Hettich).

- An up-and-coming magazine in the women's field, especially in the self-help area, is *Self* magazine published by Condé Nast. If you have a book that will fit the *Self* format and editorial content, it can be a good market for first serial sales.

- One of the fastest growing juvenile book operations is Wanderer Books at Simon & Schuster under the direction of Jack Artenstein. Artenstein became president of the juvenile and trade paperback divisions at Simon & Schuster a few years ago and has rapidly developed the juvenile division into a major factor in the industry.

- Paperback publishers are no longer impressed by movie options. This is especially true of paperback publishers who are really only interested in books that are actually sold to the movies, not just optioned.

  We could have sent our kids to college four times over with the option money I have received for books that I have represented but were never made into films.

  There is nothing wrong with having your book optioned for a film, but don't expect publishers to do handstands over the news.

- Sol Stein is not the easiest publisher in town to do business with but Stein & Day has remained vital and vibrant in good times and bad. Stein & Day is a small, aggressive firm and what makes Sol Stein particularly interesting is that he is not only a publisher but a successful novelist as well.

- Rodale Press which is located in Emmaus, Pennsylvania is the publisher of the highly successful *Prevention* magazine. Rodale also publishes some interesting self-help books, especially in the area of natural foods and organic gardening and the like. Rodale is a good market for authors who are writing books in this area.

- A good tool and research book for those who are interested in writing and want to know the best markets for their creativity is *Writer's Market.* Not only does it list all the publishers but it has an expanded section on agents. It is an indispensable tool for the writer or agent who wants to get the maximum potential for his properties.

- I don't know why it is but for some reason writers who have spent most of their lives writing for newspapers and magazines seem to have a difficult time adjusting to writing books. A successful magazine or newspaper writer does not necessarily make a successful author of books.

- If you want to join a literary or writers association, most of the major ones are listed in the *LMP* along with phone numbers, addresses and other pertinent information.

- Many literary agencies are family operations including, of course, my own and Raines & Raines, Brandt & Brandt, Arthur Pine Associates, Sanford J. Greenburger Associates, the Lescher Agency and the Scott Meredith Literary Agency, to mention but a few. By family operation, I mean, of course, that more than one member of the same family either runs the agency or works at it.

- I have never been overly impressed with the advertising agencies that specialize in book publishing. Too many of these agencies handle too many publishers with small budgets as well as publishers with large budgets, and they don't seem to have the time to give the proper creative attention to either.

  Publishers would be well served to evaluate this area because for too long too many publishers have been advertising in the same old way.

- If you are an author and you want to lecture, you will find that there are a number of excellent lecture agents around the country who are well equipped to handle authors with something to say. The lecture agencies that I would recommend looking into include in New York the Harry Walker Agency, Richard Fulton Inc., and the Keedick Lecture Bureau as well as Colston Leigh in Princeton, New Jersey and the American Program Bureau in Boston.

- If you are looking for a job with a book publishing company as an editor or in some other capacity, there are a number of employment agencies that specialize in the book industry. Some of the better known ones include the Hadle Agency, the Lynne Palmer Agency, the Mary Diehl Placement Bureau and the Remer-Ribolow Agency, all located in Manhattan.

- Jack Beaudouin, the vice president and editor of Reader's Digest Condensed Books, is one of the more important figures in book publishing. If your book is selected by the Reader's Digest Condensed Book Club, it will often mean between $30,000 and $100,000 in additional revenues although the impact of the Digest Book Club is not what it used to be. But it is still a factor in the financial success of any book.

◆ A strong area for young people in book publishing, especially women, is sales. Sales has always been and still is the backbone of the book publishing industry, and young people have a unique opportunity to learn about the industry in the best possible way—out in the field selling the product.

Unfortunately, production and art departments are not the best places to start a career in book publishing, at least not compared to sales, editorial and subsidiary rights which are all training grounds for management positions.

While the publicity departments at publishing firms can be interesting and stimulating, they are not always the road that leads to management positions. One of the exceptions to that was Sherry Arden at William Morrow who went from publicity to subsidiary rights and now is associate publisher and vice president.

There are virtually no blacks in book publishing and the industry that prides itself on being in the forefront of the defense of the Constitution has done almost nothing for the black American in terms of publishing as a real career.

You can count on the fingers of one hand the number of black editors in this town. There is really only one black editor who has any visibility and that is Toni Morrison of Random House who in addition to being a senior editor at that distinguished publishing firm is also a novelist of some note.

There are other black editors scattered among some of the major publishing firms but certainly not in the numbers that there should be.

In addition to a lack of black editors, there are no blacks that I know of in important executive positions in book publishing. There are, however, plenty of blacks in the mailrooms, stockrooms and warehouses of publishing houses.

A few months ago, Bob Bernstein, the president and chief executive officer of Random House, organized a group of publishers to publicize the plight of the Russian writer. It was obviously a wonderful gesture, but it did seem to me that the plight of the black American in book publishing was equally important.

Book publishers have done little to develop black writers in this country and that, too, is a tragedy.

Five years ago, I had a conversation with the president of a major publishing firm during which I made the suggestion that the publishing industry or one or two of the major publishing firms establish a storefront editorial office on 125th Street in the heart of Harlem. My theory was that there are talented writers walking the streets of black communities but that they are reluctant to come down town to the "lily white" publishing territory and even if they did, they wouldn't know where to begin or whom to talk to.

I felt that by establishing a storefront publishing office—right on the streets of Harlem—that we could reach the black community where they live and perhaps develop some potential talent.

I believe there is only one black literary agent functioning in book publishing. His name is Ron Hobbs and that, too, is a sad commentary on the involvement of blacks in book publishing.

American publishers have an obligation to their own and certainly the situation should be changed. Blacks, Puerto Ricans, Mexican-Americans and Indians ought to become part of the book publishing community—as editors, executives and, of course, writers.

There are many concerned and compassionate executives in book publishing who have given time and money to many causes but do little or nothing to develop minority involvement in their own industry. This is not to say that book publishers are not complying with the letter of the law which requires companies not to discriminate because of race. They are hiring blacks, but only in service areas or on the secretarial level. There are some black salesmen selling for major publishing firms but they are a very small minority of the total sales force in book publishing.

◆ The best Christmas party in publishing is the *Good Housekeeping* magazine party which is usually held at the St. Regis Hotel. Everybody who is anybody in book publishing winds up at that party, and John Mack Carter and Len Dowty are warm and gracious hosts.

◆ Two interesting trade publications worth reading quickly each month are *BP Report*, a gossipy, insiders' newsletter about the book industry with lots of items about who's doing what and who's going where, and the *West Coast Review of Books* which seems to be growing rapidly in popularity and contains not only many book reviews but also stimulating and informative articles about the industry and its people.

- Unfortunately, poetry as a category seems to be dying in bookstores. Except for an occasional book of love poetry or some other gimmicky poetry book, *real* poetry is not a money maker for publishers or authors.

- If your book is about to be published, it would be worthwhile to pop into your local bookstore and tell them about the book and offer to autograph copies that can be sold at the store. Neighborhood bookstores are usually willing to promote books for local authors. It would also be a good idea to ask your local bookstore to display the book in the window.

- Although book publishers are paying better salaries in the eighties than they did in the sixties and seventies, if you are thinking of an entry level job in book publishing and want to make a lot of money, you are probably better off working in the post office.

  Book publishing is an industry which each year gets more applicants for entry level jobs than they have positions. The publishing houses are in the buyer's seat and they are not the most generous employers for people who are just starting out.

- Two recent books which seemed to have great promise but which did not live up to expectations are *Every Secret Thing* by Patricia Hearst and *Mrs. Harris* by Diana Trilling.

  In the case of Patricia Hearst, the advance from Doubleday was supposed to have been in the neighborhood of $800,000 and in the case of Diana Trilling, not only did she receive a large advance from Harcourt, Brace Jovanovich for the book but the motion picture rights were sold for a figure represented to be over a million dollars.

  So, with these high expectations and large financial investments, why did the books fail (at least in relationship to what was expected)?

  In my judgment, it seems that when a story has already saturated the media as happened with Mrs. Harris's murder trial and with the odyssey of Patricia Hearst, the public has had enough after they have followed the stories for months in the newspapers and magazines and have watched them unfold on television.

I have always felt that stories that have been major media events do not translate well into books. Unfortunately, publishers will probably not learn the lesson of these two books and will continue to pay large advances for front page stories.

◆ Today many major authors and properties can demand a 15% royalty for their books which I think can be counterproductive. A 15% royalty usually forces the publisher to raise the price of the book and that means fewer people will buy the book.

Obviously, the 15% royalty is not the only factor in the high cost of books—printing, production, shipping, etc., all play a role—but the higher royalty rate is certainly a major reason for the spiraling cost of books. Somewhere along the line royalties will have to come down or most books will be priced totally out of reach of many people.

◆ I could never understand why publishers often schedule books and even put books in their catalogs before the manuscript is finished.

This puts a tremendous burden on not only the author but everyone connected with the book to get the manuscript into production quickly and rush the book out.

Frequently the sales force is selling books before the author is even half through writing the manuscript.

One of the reasons for this is that publishers continually need product quickly, especially if it is a book that seems to be timely.

Although I can sympathize with the publisher, I still think in most instances it is a mistake. Books should be published, not just issued. We are not talking about salami. We are talking about books and care should be given and time should be devoted to the publishing process.

Many books falter because there is not enough time to complete all the steps necessary to publishing a book properly.

When I was the editor-in-chief at Playboy Press, we published Jimmy "The Greek's" autobiography. It was a good book that Jimmy wrote with the superb collaborator Mickey Herskowitz.

Jimmy was a "hot personality" at the time (and still is today) and because of that and because Playboy needed product quickly, I rushed the process.

There is no question in my mind that Jimmy's book suffered because of that and, in addition, there were some typographical errors in the book that would not have been there if we had taken more time to properly publish the book. Jimmy "The Greek" was understandably upset and I vowed never to let that happen again if I could prevent it.

If an author feels that he is being rushed, he should stand his ground and not be panicked by an editor or publisher who insists the book must be finished overnight because the sales force is already placing the book in bookstores.

22

Book Publishing —

Where Does It Go from Here?

If I were asked to analyze the future of book publishing, the report would have to be both gloomy and optimistic. As the old joke goes, "I've got good news and bad—which do you want to hear first?"

As far as book publishing is concerned, let's take the good news first. If you are a writer, agent, editor or book publisher, the industry offers unlimited opportunities that have never been offered before. Book publishing is a much more exciting, dynamic and creative business than it was in the forties, fifties and sixties. Agents, editors and publishers are much more receptive to new ideas than they ever were before.

In times gone by, book publishers considered themselves part of a "gentlemen's industry" where old ties and button-down shirts symbolized a profession that was steeped in tradition. That's no longer so. Most of the old hands in book publishing have either retired, sold out, died or left the industry. The new people who are today the leaders in book publishing are younger, stronger and more willing to take chances.

In an industry where traditional fiction and nonfiction were once the order of the day, the changes have been notable. The best example I can give of that relates to my own experiences. A little over ten years ago, *Time* magazine ran a short piece about my publishing activities and in the story they described me as "the king of the nonbooks."

Even today the word "nonbook" needs an explanation and in those days it was almost unheard of. Actually, a nonbook is easy to describe. It is a book that has no beginning, no middle or end but is rather a product between two covers. To read a nonbook, you don't have to start on page one and continue through in sequence to the end but rather you can open the book anywhere. *The Official Preppy Handbook*, which has sold close to a million copies and is published by Workman Press, is an excellent example of a nonbook. You can start *The Official Preppy Handbook* on page forty or page sixty or page eighty-two without having to go back to page one for continuity.

My own series of books, *Kids' Letters from Camp, Kids' Letters to the Presidents* and the *Wit Series* are three examples of successful nonbooks.

When *Time* referred to me ten years ago as the "king of the nonbook," what they were really trying to say was that a new type of book was beginning to take shape. And that has been very true. The growth of the nonbook has been the most dramatic example of the changes that have taken place in book publishing. Fifteen years ago, if you offered a nonbook to a respectable publisher, he would either laugh you out of the office or explain to you gently but firmly that this is not what book publishing is all about. They would have gone on to say that book publishing is the business of literature. Book publishing is still the business of literature but it isn't the total business any longer.

There are opportunities today in book publishing that have never existed before. Virtually anything can be published as long as it does not border on the extremes of bad taste.

In a way, Bill Adler Books was partially responsible for the growth of the nonbook era but we are not alone any more. Even the most conservative and respected publishers are now always willing to discuss a nonbook or an unusual book idea that has never been tried before.

It isn't just that book publishers today are more receptive to new ideas or that they are willing to try anything, it is that the entire approach to marketing books has changed significantly. Publishers are more aware of packaging a book by developing a marketing approach for the book long before it is published and planning the elements of promotion and merchandising before the book arrives in the bookstores. Fifteen or twenty years ago the only marketing publishers were ever concerned about was the number of "quotes" they could secure for the book prior to its publication.

Twenty-five years ago television was not taken seriously in terms of promoting a book, and the entire approach to promoting and advertising a book revolved around the *New York Times* and *The Saturday Review of Literature*.

If you are someone with ideas and know how to execute them, then the possibilities in book publishing today are limitless. There's not anything that can't be done and this is in an industry that for so many years lagged behind the times.

I can remember when I offered *The Kennedy Wit* to a major book publisher and his reply was "That's just a magazine article." How often I used to hear that line. The success of *The Kennedy Wit* and the success of other book ideas which were once described as "only magazine articles" by book publishers has created a new ballgame.

In book publishing in the eighties, the idea is as important as the execution and it may seem to be just a magazine article, but if it is executed with creativity, it can be made into a successful nonfiction book.

This does not mean to say that the quality of the words doesn't count. Of course, it does. But the change has been in the receptivity of book publishers and the buying public for almost anything that is between covers.

Ideas have become more important than ever before and the ability of the publisher to promote the idea when it is published has become paramount. Techniques that were once applicable only to advertising and marketing have now become applicable to book publishing. Although it is not true of all books or even a majority of the books published, a healthy percentage of them are now merchandised, promoted and advertised the way they really should be—with creativity and vigor.

It would have been unheard of twenty years ago for a young woman like Lisa Birnbach just out of college to have edited a book like *The Official Preppy Handbook*. The success of *The Official Preppy Handbook* is an example not only of the growth of the nonbook market but an indication that a book can become virtually an industry in itself.

There are now "Preppy" T-shirts, calendars and stationery—all spin-offs from the *Preppy Handbook*. This is not an isolated case. There is a growing list of book properties which have been spun-off to games and other merchandise, all of which accrue royalties and income for the creators and the publishers.

Perhaps the most dramatic change in book retailing over the past ten years has been the growth—and I mean the spectacular growth—of the book chains.

The B. Dalton and Waldenbooks stores are a prime example. Today Dalton and Waldenbooks have a total of 1,115 stores with Dalton contributing 475 to that total and Waldenbooks contributing 640. Both Dalton and Waldenbooks are owned by major conglomerates. B. Dalton is owned by Dayton Hudson and Waldenbooks by Carter Hawley Hale.

Book publishing at the retail level used to be a business of "mom and pop stores" with the exception of some book chains like Doubleday and Brentano's which don't come near the size of Dalton and Waldenbooks.

The phenomenal growth of Dalton and Waldenbooks is even more arresting when you consider that most industry experts believe that the chains led by Dalton and Waldenbooks will control well over 60 percent of the retail book business by the year 1985. If a book makes it big at Dalton's or Walden's its chances of making it big around the country are much greater.

Dalton's has its own bestseller list and that list is watched with almost the same anticipation by book publishers as the *New York Times* Best Sellers list. If Dalton and Waldenbooks get behind a book, it is equal to an appearance on "Donahue" or any other big publicity or promotion break. They have that kind of power.

There has also been an interesting growth in the discount book field led by Barnes & Noble. Books sold at discount have become extremely popular with the book buying public, especially since the prices for hardcover books and, for that matter, trade and mass market paperbacks have increased substantially. The days of the five-dollar hardcover book are long gone and sixty-cent paperbacks are a distant memory. Printing costs have sky-rocketed in book publishing as has everything else that goes into the cost of books from advances to editorial costs to postage and publishers' overhead.

Only recently, The Newmarket Press, a new publishing firm headed by Esther Margolis who was vice president at Bantam Books, published a new hardcover edition of Jacqueline Susann's *Valley of the Dolls* to coincide with the fifteenth anniversary of its original publication. The price on Newmarket's special edition was $5.95, the same price that Bernard Geis Associates charged for the book when it first came out. Try to think of a hardcover book published today for $5.95 and you won't come up with one.

The book buying public is beginning to rebel against the high price of books, especially when a novel of 250 pages can in many instances cost over $10. The book buyer knows that if he waits six months to a year, he can buy the book at $2.95 in paperback.

The most aggressive retail establishment in the book field is Barnes & Noble. You can buy hardcover books at the Barnes & Noble bookstores at discounts ranging from 20 percent to 50 percent of the publishers' retail prices. There are twenty Barnes & Noble stores in New York, Boston and Cleveland and many more Barnes & Noble stores will open within the next few months.

Even more important than the Barnes & Noble discount chain is the Pickwick Booksellers which is a subsidiary of B. Dalton. B. Dalton plans to open hundreds of Pickwick discount stores around the country, and so the Pickwick stores, combined with Barnes & Noble and other discount chains like the Crown Books stores, will seriously affect the retail business of bookstores and chains that sell books at the publishers' list price.

There will most certainly be a price war in the near future at the retail level among the major bookstores around the country and especially among the discount chains. The obvious beneficiary of the growth of the discount bookstores will be the book buying public who will have the opportunity to buy their books at considerable savings.

The bad news about book publishing today and in the future is that there are too many books being published.

There are over 30,000 books published in hardcover every year and the publishers' lists keep growing. It is almost impossible for bookstores and the buying public to keep up with the number of books published every year. Bookstores are swamped with merchandise and the potential book buyer is bewildered by the enormous number of titles that are published every day, every month and every year.

Periodically, the presidents of the major publishing firms announce that the industry has to cut down on the number of hardcover books produced every year, but no one seems to want to take the first step.

Look at these startling statistics. Here are five of the major book publishers and the number of hardcover titles that they published in 1981.

Random House	610
Doubleday	500
Simon & Schuster	331
William Morrow	285
The Putnam Publishing Group	110

It is reasonable to ask why the bookstores take on all these books if there are so many titles published every year. The answer is, of course, that the bookstores buy most books from the publishers on consignment. That is, most unsold books are fully returnable to the publisher.

I have been involved with more than one book where the initial advance sale to the bookstores was 30,000 to 40,000 books and nine months later the stores returned to the publisher eight out of every ten books they had originally ordered.

If books were not fully returnable to the publishers, then the stores would be more judicious about the number of books they initially ordered.

The problem is even more serious in paperback publishing which is responsible for over 10,000 titles a year. Frequently cartons of paperback books sent to the bookstores are not even opened before they are returned to the publisher.

Because of the remarkable growth of product in book publishing, most authors find that their books are competing not only with the big bestsellers but with 30,000 other books which seriously affects the opportunity for their book to succeed.

Out of the 30,000 books published every year in hardcover, it is my guess that only 1,000 really make it at the retail level and that works out to less than 5 percent.

Book publishers have to have books for their salesmen to sell which is one of the reasons they are continually feeding the pipeline. But unless the industry as a whole cuts back on the number of books published every year, everybody is going to suffer, especially the authors who in some instances have devoted three to four years of their lives writing a book only to learn that they are lucky if 5,000 copies are bought.

That is definitely bad news for the industry—and bad news for the public.

It would only be fair, however, to conclude this book on an optimistic note, and the truth is that with all of its problems and growing pains and changes in the market that I have referred to throughout this book, book publishing is still an exciting and viable industry with great opportunities for growth and for people who want to make a career with the printed word.

America (and the world for that matter) is going through a communications explosion and there is no question in my mind that the business of publishing books will be in the forefront and will maintain its position of leadership.

APPENDIX

The following book proposal is a good example of a book outline that was sold. This book has just been published by William Morrow.

BOOK PROPOSAL

GETTING INTO THE UNDERGROUND ECONOMY:

A Guide to Your Family's Economic, Social and Spiritual Survival

after the Collapse of 1984-85

BY

Larry Burkett & William Proctor

Summary: Larry Burkett, a self-made multimillionaire and director of a national nonprofit financial counseling service based in Atlanta, has devoted the last decade to developing *economic "fallout shelters"*—or personal financial programs to help individuals protect themselves from a monetary cataclysm which he expects to strike in 1984 or 1985.

His basic theory—which he'll substantiate through scientific analyses, as well as concrete illustrations and anecdotes he has gathered around the country—is that there exists an *underground economy,* which most Americans are only vaguely aware of, but which they must plug into if they hope to survive and thrive after the coming collapse. Burkett's highly practical and opinionated advice about how to enter this hidden economy will include a comprehensive discussion of how a person should deal right now with concrete problems like debt and credit, secondary jobs, key investments and community-support networks.

Only by taking certain immediate protective steps can you be reasonably certain that you'll emerge intact from the impending stagflation-depression. Burkett expects the collapse to transform large segments of our national economy from a modified free enterprise system into a tightly controlled, quasi-fascist state, and only those who have anticipated and prepared for the disaster will come out unscathed.

All this may sound highly pessimistic, but Burkett isn't the stereotypical doom-and-gloom prognosticator. As he puts it, "There is a philosophy currently going around that you should buy yourself some gold, a year's worth of food and a gun to shoot your neighbor with if he tries to take what you've hoarded. But I don't believe in that approach because, for one thing, it's immoral, and for another, it just won't work."

Larry Burkett does have a negative outlook about the future of our existing economy. But at the same time he's *highly positive* about your chances for surviving in style if you get into the underground economy and start preparing solid economic fallout shelters for your family. He describes himself as a "positive-thinking realist." And this book will reflect that basic optimism, which is tempered by a recognition of those dangerous economic trends that are moving us inexorably toward a new national order.

The Authors: LARRY BURKETT is a highly successful entrepreneur, financial counselor and author who made his fortune by building and then selling a substantial minority interest in a manufacturing company.

The holder of degrees in marketing and finance, he first ran a business group for General Electric which required him to buy new businesses for the huge corporation. Then, he helped start an electronics manufacturing company, sold the business for several million dollars, and went into nonprofit financial counseling for the international Christian organization, Campus Crusade for Christ.

He next founded his own nonprofit financial counseling agency, Christian Financial Concepts, which has a mailing list of 25,000 and requires him or his staff members to speak to about 25,000 people each year through more than 60 live lectures and 600 video tape seminars. He is also embarking on a radio series that will take him to 175 stations around the country.

Finally, Burkett has written two books, *Your Finances in Changing Times* ($2.95 paperback) which has sold about 200,000 copies, and *What Husbands Wish Their Wives Knew about Money* ($1.95 paperback) which has sold about 90,000.

WILLIAM PROCTOR, a graduate of Harvard College (*magna cum laude* in history) and Harvard Law School, is a former *New York Daily News* writer-reporter who has written individually, co-authored or ghostwritten sixteen books. His most recent work includes books written for Pat Boone (*Pray to Win*, G. P. Putnam, 1980) and Art Linkletter (*Yes, You Can!*, Simon & Schuster, 1979), and a book co-authored with an astronomer-theologian entitled *The Return of the Star of Bethlehem* (Doubleday, 1980). Proctor is also co-founder and editor of Church Business Report, a national consumer and financial advice newsletter for pastors and churches.

Tentative Chapter Outline:

PART ONE: THE COMING MONEY WAR

Chapter One: The Money War Scenario

Because of incompetence in the way the federal government has managed (1) the money supply, and (2) its spending programs, it's likely that we'll soon be facing a 30% inflation rate. To control this dramatic price rise, the government will step in with extensive wage and price controls which will stay in effect for about a year and a half. These controls will cause shortages and restrict the flow of essential goods, even into areas where they are needed badly and where there is considerable demand. The government will finally realize it has to release the controls, and all the inflation that has been artificially held back will explode.

"I believe we could easily jump to 100% a year inflation at this point," Burkett says. The result will be what might be called a monetary collapse in about 1984 or 1985, where banks will close, businesses will fail and myriads of other economic disasters, including food riots, will occur.

Chapter Two: The New Economic Order: 1985 and Beyond

As a result of the monetary collapse, the government will have no choice but to assume control of the economy through the 1964 Economic Stabilization Act. Banks, businesses and even individual citizens will fall under a system of federal controls that this nation has never known before. "Things will be so bad you'll have to have a license to buy or sell your own home, get a raise and even move from one city to another," Burkett says.

The only things that might change this scenario would be (1) a complete breakdown of our system because of a failure of the government to act quickly enough to counteract the collapse and quell the riots, or (2) a war, which could delay everything for about three to four years.

For those inclined toward biblical prophecy, at least parts of this scenario are not so different from the economic controls described in Revelation 13:17, which predicts an era when government approval will be required to buy and sell goods.

Chapter Three: How Can You and Your Family Survive—and Thrive?

The only way to make it through this crisis intact is to be (1) debt-free; (2) independent of the current economic system through participation in the "underground economy"; and (3) involved in some community-support network that can help you overcome financial problems that for some reason you can't solve alone. An overview of the personal economic programs a family should follow in order to survive and thrive.

PART TWO: THE UNDERGROUND ECONOMY

Chapter Four: What's the Underground Economy and How Can You Enter It?

Description of the "underground economy" as an already-existing network of unusual trade and cost-cutting devices that few Americans understand. This economy has several "entrances" by which you can tap its vast resources. We'll introduce these entry points here and discuss them in great detail throughout this book.

Discussion of how the lower, middle and upper economic classes can each take advantage of the underground economy in their own distinctive ways.

Chapter Five: Short-Term Survival

When the monetary collapse occurs and riots start to break out, it will be essential for the prepared family to have sufficient supplies of food and other necessities to last them about three to four weeks. It's not necessary to have a six months' supply of food and an arsenal of weapons and ammunition, as some have suggested, because if the system breaks down to the extent that there is chaos for several months, it probably won't matter how much food or ammunition you have. Checklist of the basic goods you'll need and a few practical suggestions for preserving your family's safety during this transition period.

Chapter Six: The Gold Illusion and Other Fallacies

The new economic order will be a cashless society, and there's a great likelihood that gold (and possibly silver) will be outlawed as a private investment or medium of exchange. Other investments and personal financial practices to stay away from.

Chapter Seven: The Bare-Bones Budget Principle

How families at different economic levels can reorganize their budgets to prepare most effectively for the coming collapse. Little-known ways to cut costs. Examples: A young couple can buy a refurbished house, moved from redeveloped land, for about $10 a square foot, even though building a new house will cost about $40 to $50 a square foot. Also, you can save 10% right off the top of your food budget by certain methods of buying items in bulk. Many other examples from Burkett's travels around the country will be included.

Chapter Eight: Working Underground

One of the best investments—and methods of preparing for the coming hyper-inflation and collapse—is to learn an occupational skill in addition to your regular job. If you're plugged into the labor market, even on a part-time basis, your fees and wages will go up as prices do and will provide a much better hedge against inflation than most investments.

Profiles of what types of people do best in certain types of part-time employment. Examples: Would you make a good Amway or similar independent sales representative or distributor? Burkett can identify quite accurately the types of people who succeed and fail in this sort of selling business. Also, illustrations of other secondary work, such as a pastor who manufactures solar collectors from plywood boxes during his spare time. "A solar manufacturing company pays him $100 apiece for them, and he makes about two a week," Burkett explains. "It's his hobby."

We'll also describe various ways that lower-income individuals can get started in a part-time, inflation-hedge type business which will carry them through the collapse—but which will require little or no up-front capital to get started.

Chapter Nine: Surviving without Money

There are a number of individuals, community organizations and churches around the country that have been exploring the concept of trading goods and services without using money as a means of exchange. This practice, which in some ways is a return to the ancient economic principle of bartering, is a key element in the underground economy which Burkett has identified. Discussion of the ways you can begin to develop a moneyless network of exchange right now, without incurring any tax consequences. Examples of groups which have set up a special system of credits, rather than money, to exchange goods and services with friends. In this way, they reduce their personal expenditures and their need to rely on the increasingly worthless money being issued by the government.

Chapter Ten: How to Make and Keep a Fortune in Hard Times

This will be a lengthy chapter (and may eventually be subdivided into several chapters) on the best approaches to personal investment to prepare for the lean years ahead. Special emphasis will be placed on the best investments for people at different income levels. (E.g., right now, the Bank of England pays about 23% annual interest on short-term money instruments, but the required minimum investment is $10,000—a figure that's high enough to exclude many people in the lower and middle income groups.) In general, Burkett is positive about putting your money into real estate, some collectibles like precious jewels, and gas wells; but he's negative about gold, oil wells, and most bank accounts.

PART THREE: AFTER THE COLLAPSE

Chapter Eleven: You Can't Survive Alone!—Your Community after the Collapse

Burkett feels it's impossible for any individual or family to survive the coming economic collapse in isolation. A membership in some sort of supportive community is absolutely essential if you hope to take full advantage of bartering and sharing essential goods, finding job opportunities, and utilizing other services. Communal groups may also be forced temporarily to take on the role of defense organizations as law and order break down in various parts of the country.

Description of basic elements in an effective support community. These include the same spiritual or philosophical assumptions among members of the group; a diversity of economic skills; and a family-like commitment of members to one another. Current models are the Israeli kibbutz, the Mormon Church and various church programs and Christian communities, which will be discussed in detail.

Chapter Twelve: Conclusion: Profile of a Survivor

Burkett feels that the reason we've gotten into the difficulties we're now facing is that "we're no longer a nation of fighters." But those who survive in style through the impending cataclysm will have to demonstrate some of those tough inner qualities of independence, perseverance, faith and resilience that characterized the first American settlers and frontiersmen. We'll conclude with a detailed description of the type of men and women who can expect to come out on top after the collapse.

HOW TO TELL DOUBLEDAY ABOUT YOUR BOOK

We are interested in the work of new, unknown, or little known writers. We ask that you send us first a letter (not your manuscript) so that we can save your time—and ours.

Your letter of inquiry should be addressed to the Editorial Department 195, Doubleday Publishing Co., 245 Park Avenue, New York, N. Y. 10167.

The letter may be as short as one page, but no longer than six pages, and, always, typed (doublespaced), please.

In the first sentence, tell us whether your book is a novel, a biography, a mystery, a cookbook, or whatever.

The first paragraph should give us an idea of what your book is about. A clear and straightforward description is fine.

If your book is a novel, please give us a brief summary of the plot and background, and a quick sketch of the major characters.

The letter should be accompanied by a sample of your writing from the proposed book. This sample should be not more than ten pages in length, and, if it is to be returned, a properly addressed manila envelope, with sufficient postage affixed, should be enclosed. *Do* keep a copy for yourself, of course.

If you have been published, give us details. Tell us of any credentials or experience that particularly qualify you to write your book. For a nonfiction book, it will be helpful to consult the *Subject Guide to Books in Print* (available in most libraries) so that you are aware of other books on the same or similar subjects and can tell us how your book differs from them.

Please do not submit more than one query at a time.

Finally, letters of inquiry are more welcome, obviously, if clean and typed with a good ribbon. If we ask to see your manuscript, it should be submitted doublespaced on white paper. Please retain a carbon copy, since we cannot assume responsibility for loss or damage to manuscripts. Sufficient postage, in the form of loose stamps, should accompany your submission to insure the return of your manuscript in the event it is not accepted for publication.

Good luck—and thank you for being interested in Doubleday.

DOUBLEDAY & CO., INC.
Editorial Department

AUTHOR/AGENT AGREEMENT

The author agrees to send the agency his entire writing output, and turn over to it all related items such as anthology, reprint, or other offers which may come up; and the agency agrees to expend its best efforts to sell the author's work at best possible rates. For this, the agency will receive a commission of 10% on all American sales and 20% on foreign sales, and it is agreed that commissions as listed shall be due and paid immediately by author on all sales made during the term of representation whether such sales are actually consummated by the agency or the author.

Both agree that the relationship may be ended at any time by mutual consent, but that, if either wishes it, the relationship will remain in force for two years from above date. If either wishes the relationship to end at the conclusion of the two year period, he will write and so state prior to the 15th day of the final month, and the relationship will end automatically on the final day of the final month; but if neither so writes, this agreement will extend automatically for an additional two years, and the same applies every two years thereafter. Notwithstanding the foregoing, however, the relationship may not be ended if author is indebted to the agency for disbursements, charges, or other monies of any kind; the agency will notify the author of indebtedness, if any, at the time of mutual consent to end the relationship, or upon receipt of the author's notification that he is ending the relationship at the conclusion of a two year period, but the relationship will end only when such indebtedness is repaid by the author in full.

If the relationship ends, the agency agrees to return the author's unsold scripts as rapidly as possible and attach a full list of rejecting markets to each script. It is mutually agreed, however, that the agency will continue to represent in perpetuity all subsidiary rights to all properties on which the agency made the initial sale during its term of representation of the author.

____

Author

____

Agent

AUTHOR/AGENT CONTRACT

The author hereby irrevocably designates Bill Adler Books Inc., 551 Fifth Avenue, New York, N. Y. 10017 the author's sole and exclusive agent in connection with any and all matters directly or indirectly relating to the Work or to this agreement or any other agreement entered into by the author or on the author's behalf with reference to the Work. All payments due or to become due to the author hereunder shall be made to and in the name of said agent who is hereby irrevocably authorized to give receipt for same on the author's behalf. The author agrees to pay and does hereby irrevocably designate the author's said agent to receive and retain fifteen percent (15%) of any and all monies payable to the author in respect of the Work, including but not limited to monies payable to the author under this agreement or any other agreement entered into by the author or on the author's behalf with reference to the Work.

California Based Literary Agents

Adams, Ray & Rosenberg—Los Angeles
Albert Literary Agency—Aptos, CA
Ned Brown, Inc.—Beverly Hills
Linda Chester Literary Agency, La Jolla, CA
Ruth Cohen Literary Agency—Menlo Park, CA
Shirley Collier Agency—Los Angeles
Cosay, Werner & Associates—Beverly Hills
Eisenbach-Greene-Duchow—Los Angeles
Reece Halsey Agency, Los Angeles
Mitchell Hamilburg Agency, Beverly Hills
Heacock Literary Agency, Venice, CA
Adele Horwitz, San Francisco
Independent Publishers Services/The Gottstein Co., San Francisco
Kahlenberg Associates, Santa Monica
Michael Larsen/Elizabeth Pomada—San Francisco
Julian Portman Agency, Hollywood
Martha Sternberg, San Francisco
Teal & Watt Literary Agency, Fullerton, CA

The cast of celebrities and "brand names" that we have either represented, co-agented, packaged or caused to be published is impressive. The list includes:

Steve Allen
Wally Amos ("Famous Amos")
Gene Autry
Baskin-Robbins
Dr. Herbert Benson
George Blanda
Bill Boggs
Pat Boone
Boy Scouts of America
John Mack Carter
Lillian Carter
Suzy Chaffee
Ralph Charell
Dick Clark
Rosemary Clooney
Herb Cohen
William Cohen, U. S. Senator
Howard Cosell
Buster Crabbe
Morton Dean
Phil Donahue
Dan Dorfman
Mrs. William O. Douglas
Hugh Downs
Paul Duke
Educational Testing Service
Evelyn Wood Reading Dynamics
Barry Farber
Dr. Frank Field
Frank Ford
Helen Forrest
Dr. George Gallup, Jr.
General Nutrition Corporation
Phyllis George
Charles Goren
Virginia Graham
Lorne Greene
Monty Hall
Frank Harden
Gary Hart, U. S. Senator
Dr. Henry Heimlich
Lenore Hershey
Mrs. Gordie Howe
Dr. Arnold Hutschnecker
Institute for Human Nutrition at Columbia University
Michael Jackson
Jacoby and Meyers
Eliot Janeway
Leon Jaworski
Esther Jungreis
Myron Kandel
Thelma Kandel
Captain Kangaroo
Larry King
Janet Langhart
Arthur Levitt, Jr.
Doris Lilly
Art Linkletter
Joan Lunden
Robert MacNeil
The MacNeil/Lehrer Report
Irving Mansfield
Marjorie Margolies
Willie Mays
Pat McMillen
Bernard Meltzer
Miss Teenage America
Bess Myerson
Ralph Nader
Ron Nessen
New York Stock Exchange, Inc.
Charles Osgood
Drew Pearson
Jack Perkins
Wally Phillips
Francine Prince
The Public Citizen Group
Dan Rather
Nancy Reagan

Ronald Reagan
Steve Reeves
Lyn Revson
Geraldo Rivera
Romper Room
James Roosevelt
Wilma Rudolph
William Rusher
William Safire
Dr. Lee Salk
Jessica Savitch
John Scheuer
Willard Scott
Jimmy "The Greek" Snyder
Paul Sorvino
Mark Spitz
Stanley Kaplan Educational Center
Gale Storm
John Cameron Swayze
Nancy Thurmond
Gene Tierney
Margaret Truman
Admiral Stansfield Turner
Bob Uecker
United States Military Academy
Mike Wallace
Jack Weaver
Dr. Myron Winick
Warner Wolf
Dr. Sidney Wolfe

INDEX